GENEALOGIST'S HANDBOOK FOR NEW ENGLAND RESEARCH

Second Edition

Edited by

Marcia Wiswall Lindberg

NEW ENGLAND HISTORIC GENEALOGICAL SOCIETY

Boston   1985

First Edition published by the
NEW ENGLAND LIBRARY ASSOCIATION
(Bibliography Committee)
1980

c1985 by NEW ENGLAND HISTORIC GENEALOGICAL SOCIETY
ISBN: 0-88082-011-X

Printed by
PRINTCRAFT
of Wilmington, Mass.

Order From:

New England Historic Genealogical Society
Sales Department
101 Newbury Street
Boston, Massachusetts 02116

PREFACE

The Genealogists Handbook for New England Research was conceived as a guide for persons tracing their family roots in New England. It is not a "How-to" book, but rather a location guide to public records, depositories, libraries and genealogical societies in New England.

The first edition of the Genealogists Handbook was published in 1980 under the auspices of the New England Library Association. The original material was compiled by the NELA Bibiliography Committee, with Marcia Wiswall as chairperson. Serving on the Committee were: Laura P. Abbott, Robert Charles Anderson, Duane E. Crabtree, David C. Dearborn, Joan S. Hayden, Thomas J. Kemp, Karen M. Light and Denis J. Lesieur. Six printings (6,000 copies) of the 1980 edition were sold out by 1984 when the New England Library Association transferred copyright privileges to the New England Historic Genealogical Society.

The present volume was edited and prepared by Marcia Wiswall Lindberg, who guided the first edition. Requests for updated information, sent to all 284 agencies listed in the first edition, resulted in more than 200 corrections and additions. This edition also contains a new alphabetical list of towns in Vermont.

ARRANGEMENT

The arrangement is alphabetical by state and then by record type within the state. Under each state is listed:

VITAL RECORDS (births, marriages and deaths)

CENSUS RECORDS (United States and State Censuses)

PROBATE RECORDS   (Wills, administrations, divorces, etc.)

LAND RECORDS (Registration of Deeds)

CEMETERY RECORDS (Locations of cemetery records)

CHURCH RECORDS (If significant)

MILITARY RECORDS (Federal and State)

IMMIGRATION RECORDS (if applicable)

LIBRARIES   (with significant or unique genealogical holdings)

GENEALOGICAL SOCIETIES

JOURNALS, PERIODICALS AND NEWSLETTERS

BOOKS AND ARTICLES

ACKNOWLEDGEMENTS

Appreciation is extended to the following people for their assistance in preparing this edition of the Genealogists Handbook:

Ann Barry and Elizabeth Abbe for the section on Connecticut
Danny D. Smith, Justice David Nichols and Ellen Goodale for the section
    on Maine
David C. Dearborn for the sections on Massachusetts and New Hampshire.
Jane C. Fiske for the section on Rhode Island
Alice Eichholz for the section on Vermont.

Special gratitude is extended to Robert Charles Anderson of Salt Lake City (formerly of Belchertown, Mass.) who proofread the entire manuscript.

Appreciation is acknowledged also to the public officials who answered our request for updated material; to Marjorie Potter of the Lynnfield Public Library Staff for proofreading; to Edward W. Hanson for his editorial assistance, and to Dr. Ralph J. Crandall, Director of the New England Historic Genealogical Society who agreed to publish this revised edition.

The present volume was prepared by the Editor, using an IBM PC and an NEC 3530 Spinwriter with Elite type. Notification of errors or omissions may be sent to the New England Historic Genealogical Society at 101 Newbury Street, Boston, MA 02116.

Marcia Wiswall Lindberg
Editor

Lynnfield, Massachusetts
June 1985

CONNECTICUT

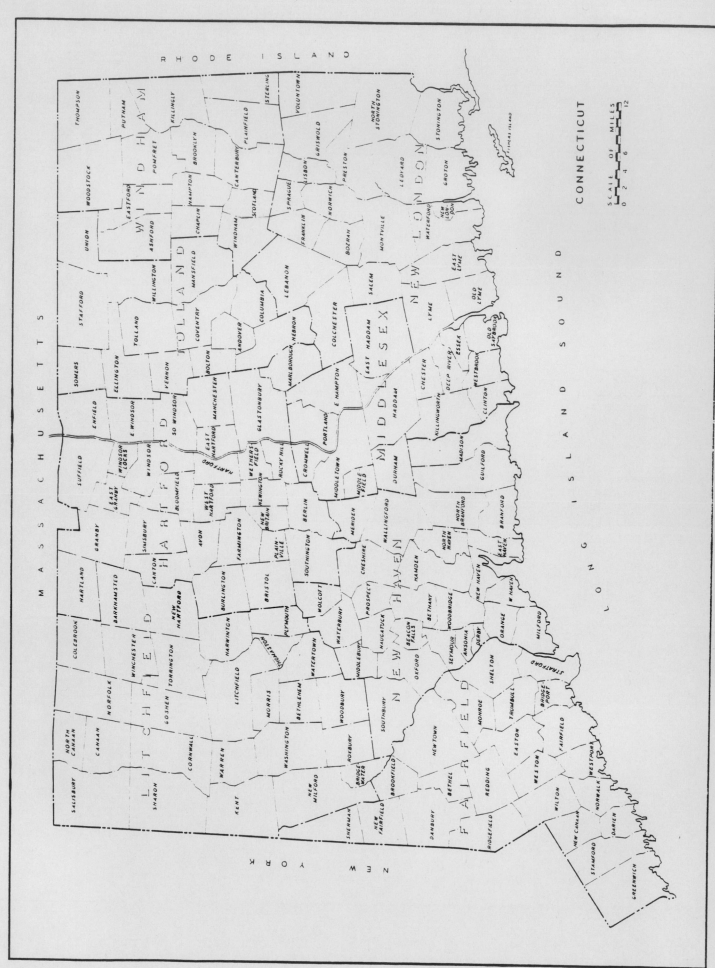

CONNECTICUT

CONNECTICUT

Connecticut is a gold mine for genealogists and local historians. It is a small compact state with records which have been generally well preserved from its earliest days. For the genealogist, the stepping off point for research is the Connecticut State Library in Hartford. Its library has thousands of valuable historical and genealogical reference books and periodicals and it houses the state archives. The records and indexes for genealogical use there are among the best and most centralized in the country.

THE CONNECTICUT STATE LIBRARY
231 Capitol Avenue
Hartford, CT 06106
203-566-3692 or 3690
Mon-Fri 8:30 to 5
Sat 9 to 1 (except
  holiday weekends)

Directions: I-91 North to Capitol exit. Take connector to end at traffic circle. Straight across to Elm Street. Left on Trinity St. to Capitol Ave. I-91 South to I-84 West, Asylum Ave. exit. Right on Asylum, left onto Broad St., left on Capitol Avenue. I-84 East to Capitol Ave. exit. Left on Capitol Ave. On-street parking Mon-Fri. Staff lot available on Saturday. Within walking distance of train & bus stations.

Facilities: Lunch room in Library. Self-operated photocopying $.10. Several microfilm readers. Two reader/printers $.25. Limited reference service by mail. Cannot search printed genealogies or do extensive research. Will supply photocopies @ $.25 per page and/or photostats @ $5 - $6.50 per page. Materials do not circulate. Interlibrary Loan requests granted only for general histories, biography, and duplicate copies of local histories and genealogies.

Holdings: Extensive collection of local histories and genealogies for New England and especially Connecticut. Unique statewide records indexes to vital records from Connecticut towns up to 1850; selected Connecticut church records; family Bible records; newspaper marriage and death records 1755-about 1870; cemetery inscriptions to about 1933; probate records. The Library also has Federal census records, microfilm land records to 1850, military service records, county court records, manuscript genealogies, maps, clippings files, photograph files and state government archives.

Publications:
  Checklist of Probate Records in The Connecticut State Library, 1981.
  Guide to the Archives in the Connecticut State Library, 1981.
  List of Church Records in the Connecticut State Library, 1976.
  Records of the Judicial Department (Part A): Court Records in the
      Connecticut State Library, 1636-1945, 1977.
  Historical and Genealogical Materials in the Connecticut State Library, 1982.
  Guide to Genealogical Materials in the Connecticut State Library, 1984, is
      designed for visitors to the library.
  "Historical and Genealogical Materials..." is available free upon request.

****

VITAL RECORDS

Each Connecticut town has kept its own vital records from its settlement to the present and they may be consulted in the town halls. Researchers should also know that abstracts of most of the town vital records, down to 1850, are housed in the Connecticut State Library in what is called the Barbour Collection. (See list of towns under Connecticut - Probate and Land Records.)

In the Barbour Collection, the Town Vital Records are arranged alphabetically, by individual, on a state-wide basis. The coverage years vary from town to town. Microfilm copies have also been made of the Barbour Collection, making it accessible to residents outside of Connecticut. (Copies may be purchased by institutions from: Genealogical Department, Library of the Church of Jesus Christ of Latter-day Saints, 50 East North Temple, Salt Lake City, UT 84150. Permission must be obtained from the Connecticut State Library.)

Vital Records after 1850 are available only in the town offices, and, after 1897, they are still recorded on the town level but are centralized at the State Department of Health as well. (Full certified copy: $3 payable to the Connecticut Department of Health Services.) The Vital Records to 1900 are being filmed and placed at the State Library and will be available through LDS stake libraries.

STATE OF CONNECTICUT
Department of Health Services
OFFICE OF PUBLIC HEALTH
150 Washington Street
Hartford, CT 06106

Directions: I-91 North to Capitol exit. Take connector to end at traffic circle. Straight across to Elm Street. Left on Trinity St., across intersection to Washington St.

Note: Connecticut law allows access to vital records for members of legally incorporated genealogical societies. This is interpreted by the Attorney General as societies incorporated in Connecticut, such as The Connecticut Society of Genealogists, Stamford Genealogical Society, Inc., and Middlesex Genealogical Society.

****

CENSUS RECORDS - FEDERAL

Copies of all of the Federal Census schedules for Connecticut from 1790 to 1880, 1900 and 1910 are available to the public. The 1890 census was destroyed. The CONNECTICUT STATE LIBRARY has a card file index to all of the schedules from 1790-1850. These same years have also been indexed by commercial firms, such as Accelerated Indexing Systems, Inc. of Bountiful, Utah, and are available in book form at the CONNECTICUT HISTORICAL SOCIETY and a few large libraries. The State Library also has the Soundex Index on microfilm of the 1880 and the 1900 schedules for Connecticut. (The 1910 schedules have no index.)

Federal Census schedules for all states in the United States are available on microfilm at the NATIONAL ARCHIVES - BOSTON BRANCH in Waltham, Massachusetts. These schedules are also available on Interlibrary Loan from several commercial establishments.

****

CONNECTICUT

CENSUS RECORDS - STATE

Connecticut did not take any state census as such. However, there are town tax lists, state militia rolls, and other records that may be consulted for lists of Connecticut residents from Colonial times. One census taken in Connecticut that is unique in the nation is the Connecticut State Military Census of 1917. The census is a detailed record of 491,000 individuals officially including all males from ages 20 to 30 (although often including all males from 16 and up), friendly and enemy aliens, nurses, automobile owners and statistical data relating to agriculture. It is kept at the CONNECTICUT STATE LIBRARY in the STATE ARCHIVES, Record Group 29.

##

PROBATE AND LAND RECORDS

PROBATE RECORDS are recorded by the court of the local probate district. Until about 1698 the probate courts were not separated from the county courts. In 1719 a division of the four original probate districts occurred and this process of division continued until now (1984) there are 131 probate districts for Connecticut's 169 towns, as some have been established and then disestablished. The Connecticut State Library has received on deposit most probate estate papers prior to 1850 and about half of the probate estate papers up to 1900. Most are indexed by decedent and the library staff will check the index for a specific name. Pre-1880 estate papers are also available on microfilm. The State Library also has microfilm copies of probate court record books prior to 1850. Later records of both types are still in the probate courts, but the books to ca. 1900 are currently being filmed, with copies available at the State Library and LDS stake libraries.

LAND RECORDS are recorded and indexed by the town clerk of each town and may be consulted in the town halls. The Connecticut State Library has a microfilm collection containing copies of deeds, mortgages, releases and related records for most towns to the mid 1800s. The land records to ca. 1900 are currently being filmed, with copies available at the State Library and at LDS stake libraries. Grantor and grantee indexes, by town, are included but there is not a statewide index. For this reason, the library staff will photocopy material for a correspondent only if the volume and page number of the original record is supplied.

##

TOWN	TOWN EST.	PARENT TOWN	COUNTY	PROBATE DISTRICT	DATE EST.	PARENT DISTRICT
Andover	1848	Coventry Hebron	Tolland	Andover	1851	Hebron
Ansonia	1889	Derby	New Haven	Derby	1858	New Haven
Ashford	1714	----	Windham	Ashford	1830	Pomfret
Avon	1830	Farmington	Hartford	Avon	1844	Farmington
Barkhamsted	1779	----	Litchfield	Barkhamsted	1834	New Hartford
Beacon Falls	1871	Bethany Oxford Seymour Naugatuck	New Haven	Naugatuck	1863	Waterbury

TOWN	TOWN EST.	PARENT TOWN	COUNTY	PROBATE DISTRICT	DATE EST.	PARENT DISTRICT
Berlin	1785	Farmington Wethersfield Middletown	Hartford	Berlin	1824	Framington Hartford Middletown
Bethany	1832	Woodbridge	New Haven	Bethany	1854	New Haven
Bethel	1855	Danbury	Fairfield	Bethel	1859	Danbury
Bethlehem	1787	Woodbury	Litchfield	Woodbury	1719	Hartford Fairfield New Haven
Bloomfield	1835	Windsor Farmington Simsbury	Hartford	Hartford	original	----
Bolton	1720	----	Tolland	Andover	1851	Hebron
Bozrah	1786	Norwich	New London	Bozrah	1843	Norwich
Branford	1685	New Haven	New Haven	Branford	1850	Guilford
Bridgeport	1821	Stratford Fairfield	Fairfield	Bridgeport	1840	Stratford
Bridgewater	1856	New Milford	Litchfield	New Milford	1787	Woodbury Sharon Danbury
Bristol	1785	Farmington	Hartford	Bristol	1830	Farmington
Brookfield	1788	Danbury New Milford Newtown	Fairfield	Brookfield	1850	Newtown
Brooklyn	1786	Pomfret Canterbury	Windham	Brooklyn	1833	Pomfret Plainfield
Burlington	1806	Bristol	Hartford	Burlington	1834	Farmington
Canaan	1739	----	Litchfield	Canaan	1846	Sharon
Canterbury	1703	Plainfield	Windham	Canterbury	1835	Plainfield
Canton	1806	Simsbury	Hartford	Canton	1841	Simsbury
Chaplin	1822	Windham Hampton Mansfield	Windham	Chaplin	1850	Windham
Chatham (see East Hampton)				Chatham (see East Hampton)		
Cheshire	1780	Wallingford	New Haven	Cheshire	1829	Wallingford
Chester	1836	Saybrook	Middlesex	Saybrook	1780	Guilford
Clinton	1838	Killingworth	Middlesex	Clinton	1862	Killingworth
Colchester	1698	----	New London	Colchester	1832	East Haddam
Colebrook	1779	----	Litchfield	Winchester	1838	Norfolk
Columbia	1804	Lebanon	Tolland	Andover	1851	Hebron
Cornwall	1740	----	Litchfield	Cornwall	1847	Litchfield
Coventry	1712	----	Tolland	Coventry	1849	Hebron
Cromwell	1851	Middletown	Middlesex	Middletown	1752	Hartford Guilford East Haddam
Danbury	1687	----	Fairfield	Danbury	1744	Fairfield
Darien	1820	Stamford	Fairfield	Darien	1921	Stamford
Deep River	1635	----	Middlesex	Deep River	1949	Saybrook
(name of town was Saybrook until 1947)						
Derby	1675	----	New Haven	Derby	1858	New Haven
Durham	1708	----	Middlesex	Middletown	1752	Hartford Guilford East Haddam

TOWN	TOWN EST.	PARENT TOWN	COUNTY	PROBATE DISTRICT	DATE EST.	PARENT DISTRICT
Eastford	1847	Ashford	Windham	Eastford	1849	Ashford
East Granby	1858	Granby Windsor Locks	Hartford	East Granby	1865	Granby
East Haddam	1734	Haddam	Middlesex	East Haddam	1741	Hartford
East Hampton	1767	Middletown	Middlesex	East Hampton	1824	Middletown
(name of town was Chatham until 1915)						
East Hartford	1783	Hartford	Hartford	East Hartford	1887	Hartford
East Haven	1785	New Haven	New Haven	East Haven	1955	New Haven
East Lyme	1839	Lyme Waterford	New London	East Lyme	1843	New London
Easton	1845	Weston	Fairfield	Trumbull	1959	Bridgeport
(Easton, est. 1875 from Weston, was annexed to Bridgeport, 1878)						
East Windsor	1768	Windsor	Hartford	East Windsor	1782	Hartford Stafford
Ellington	1786	East Windsor	Tolland	Ellington	1826	East Windsor Stafford
Enfield	1683	----	Hartford	Enfield	1831	East Windsor
(part of Massachusetts until 1749)						
Essex	1852	Saybrook	Middlesex	Essex	1853	Saybrook
(name of town was Old Saybrook from 1852 until 1854, when a new town of Old Saybrook was separated from it. At that time the 1852 Old Saybrook changed its name to Essex.)			(name of district was Old Saybrook until 1859. Then a new probate district of Old Saybrook was established and the earlier district changed its name to Essex.)			
Fairfield	1639	----	Fairfield	Fairfield	original	----
Farmington	1645	----	Hartford	Farmington	1769	Hartford
Franklin	1786	Norwich	New London	Norwich	1748	New London
Glastonbury	1690	Wethersfield	Hartford	Glastonbury	1975	Hartford
Goshen	1739	----	Litchfield	Torrington	1847	Litchfield
Granby	1786	Simsbury	Hartford	Granby	1807	Simsbury Hartford
Greenwich	1665	Stamford	Fairfield	Greenwich	1853	Stamford
(under jurisdiction of Dutch at New Amsterdam 1642-1656)						
Griswold	1815	Preston	New London	Griswold	1979	Norwich
Groton	1705	New London	New London	Groton	1839	Stonington
Guilford	1643	----	New Haven	Guilford	1719	New Haven New London
Haddam	1668	----	Middlesex	Haddam	1830	Middletown Chatham
Hamden	1786	New Haven	New Haven	Hamden	1945	New Haven
Hampton	1786	Windham Pomfret Brooklyn Canterbury Mansfield	Windham	Hampton	1836	Windham
Hartford	1635	----	Hartford	Hartford	original	----
Hartland	1761	----	Hartford	Hartland	1836	Granby
Harwinton	1737	----	Litchfield	Harwinton	1835	Litchfield
Hebron	1708	----	Tolland	Hebron	1789	Windham East Windsor & East Haddam

CONNECTICUT

TOWN	TOWN EST.	PARENT TOWN	COUNTY	PROBATE DISTRICT	DATE EST.	PARENT DISTRICT
Huntington (see Shelton)				Huntington (see Shelton)		
Kent	1739	-----	Litchfield	Kent	1831	New Milford
Killingly	1708	-----	Windham	Killingly	1830	Pomfret Plainfield
Killingworth	1667	-----	Middlesex	Killingworth	1834	Saybrook
Lebanon	1700	-----	New London	Lebanon	1826	Windham
Ledyard	1836	Groton	New London	Ledyard	1837	Stonington
Lisbon	1786	Norwich	New London	Norwich	1748	New London
Litchfield	1719	-----	Litchfield	Litchfield	1742	Hartford Woodbury New Haven
Lyme	1667	Saybrook	New London	Lyme	1869	Old Lyme
				Lyme "Old District" (see Old Lyme District)		
Madison	1826	Guilford	New Haven	Madison	1834	Guilford
Manchester	1823	East Harford	Hartford	Manchester	1850	East Hartford
Mansfield	1702	Windham	Tolland	Mansfield	1831	Windham
Marlborough	1803	Colchester Glastonbury Hebron	Hartford	Marlborough	1846	Colchester
Meriden	1806	Wallingford	New Haven	Meridan	1836	Wallingford
Middlebury	1807	Waterbury Woodbury Southbury	New Haven	Waterbury	1779	Woodbury
Middlefield	1866	Middletown	Middlesex	Middletown	1752	Hartford Guilford East Haddam
Middletown	1651	-----	Middlesex	Middletown	1752	Hartford Guilford East Haddam
Milford	1639	-----	New Haven	Milford	1832	New Haven
Monroe	1823	Huntington	Fairfield	Trumbull	1959	Bridgeport
Montville	1786	New London	New London	Montville	1851	New London
Morris	1859	Litchfield	Litchfield	Litchfield	1742	Hartford Woodbury New Haven
Naugatuck	1844	Waterbury Bethany Oxford	New Haven	Naugatuck	1863	Waterbury
New Britain	1850	Berlin	Hartford	Berlin	1824	Farmington Hartford Middletown
New Canaan	1801	Norwalk Stamford	Fairfield	New Canaan	1937	Norwalk
New Fairfield	1740	-----	Fairfield	New Fairfield	1975	Danbury
New Hartford	1738	-----	Litchfield	New Hartford	1825	Simsbury
New Haven	1638	-----	New Haven	New Haven original		-----
Newington	1871	Wethersfield	Hartford	Newington	1975	Hartford
New London	1648	-----	New London	New London original		-----
New Milford	1712	-----	Litchfield	New Milford	1787	Woodbury Sharon Danbury

TOWN	TOWN EST.	PARENT TOWN	COUNTY	PROBATE DISTRICT	DATE EST.	PARENT DISTRICT
Newtown	1711	-----	Fairfield	Newtown	1820	Danbury
Norfolk	1758	-----	Litchfield	Norfolk	1779	Simsbury Litchfield
No. Branford	1831	Branford	New Haven	No. Branford	1937	Guilford Wallingford
North Canaan	1858	Canaan	Litchfield	Canaan	1846	Sharon
North Haven	1786	New Haven	New Haven	North Haven	1955	New Haven
No. Stonington	1807	Stonington	New London	No. Stonington	1835	Stonington
Norwalk	1651	-----	Fairfield	Norwalk	1802	Fairfield Stamford
Norwich	1662	-----	New London	Norwich	1748	New London
Old Lyme (name of town was South Lyme until 1857)	1855	Lyme	New London	Old Lyme (name of district was Lyme "old district" until 1868)	1830	New London
Old Saybrook	1854	Old Saybrook (i.e. Essex, q.v.)	Middlesex	Old Saybrook (i.e.Essex q.v.)	1859	Old Saybrook
Orange	1822	Milford New Haven	New Haven	Orange	1975	New Haven
Oxford	1798	Derby Southbury	New Haven	Oxford	1846	New Haven
Plainfield	1699	-----	Windham	Plainfield	1747	Windham
Plainville	1869	Farmington	Hartford	Plainville	1909	Farmington
Plymouth	1795	Watertown	Litchfield	Plymouth	1833	Waterbury
Pomfret	1713	-----	Windham	Pomfret	1752	Windham Plainfield
Portland	1841	Chatham	Middlesex	Portland	1913	Chatham
Preston	1687	-----	New London	Norwich	1748	New London
Prospect	1827	Cheshire Waterbury	New Haven	Cheshire	1829	Wallingford
Putnam	1855	Thompson Pomfret Killingly	Windham	Putnam	1856	Thompson
Redding	1767	Fairfield	Fairfield	Redding	1839	Danbury
Ridgefield	1709	-----	Fairfield	Ridgefield	1841	Danbury
Rocky Hill	1843	Wethersfield	Hartford	Newington	1975	Hartford
Roxbury	1796	Woodbury	Litchfield	Roxbury	1842	Woodbury
Salem	1819	Colchester Lyme Montville	New London	Salem	1841	Colchester New London
Salisbury	1741	-----	Litchfield	Salisbury	1847	Sharon
Saybrook (see Deep River)				Saybrook (serves only town of Chester)	1780	Guilford
Scotland	1857	Windham	Windham	Windham	1719	Hartford New London
Seymour	1850	Derby	New Haven	Derby	1858	New Haven
Sharon	1739	-----	Litchfield	Sharon	1755	Litchfield
Shelton (name of town was Huntington until 1919)	1789	Stratford	Fairfield	Shelton (name of district was Huntington until 1919)	1889	Bridgeport
Sherman	1802	New Fairfield	Fairfield	Sherman	1846	New Milford
Simsbury	1670	-----	Hartford	Simsbury	1769	Hartford

TOWN	TOWN EST.	PARENT TOWN	COUNTY	PROBATE DISTRICT	DATE EST.	PARENT DISTRICT
Somers	1734	Enfield	Tolland	Somers	1834	Ellington
(part of Massachusetts until 1749)						
Southbury	1787	Woodbury	New Haven	Southbury	1967	Woodbury
Southington	1779	Farmington	Hartford	Southington	1825	Farmington
South Windsor	1845	East Windsor	Hartford	East Windsor	1782	Hartford Stafford
Sprague	1861	Lisbon Franklin	New London	Norwich	1748	New London
Stafford	1719	----	Tolland	Stafford	1759	Hartford Pomfret
Stamford	1641	----	Fairfield	Stamford	1728	Fairfield
Sterling	1794	Voluntown	Windham	Sterling	1852	Plainfield
Stonington	1662	----	New London	Stonington	1766	New London
Stratford	1639	----	Fairfield	Stratford	1782	Fairfield
Suffield	1674	----	Hartford	Suffield	1821	Hartford Granby
(part of Massachusetts until 1749)						
Thomaston	1875	Plymouth	Litchfield	Thomaston	1882	Litchfield
Thompson	1785	Killingly	Windham	Thompson	1832	Pomfret
Tolland	1715	----	Tolland	Tolland	1830	Stafford
Torrington	1740	----	Litchfield	Torrington	1847	Litchfield
Trumbull	1797	Stratford	Fairfield	Trumbull	1959	Bridgeport
Union	1734	----	Tolland	Stafford	1759	Hartford Pomfret
Vernon	1808	Bolton	Tolland	Ellington	1826	East Windsor Stafford
Voluntown	1721	----	New London	Norwich	1830	Plainfield
(Voluntown est. in 1830 from Plainfield, annexed to Norwich 1889)						
Wallingford	1670	New Haven	New Haven	Wallingford	1776	New Haven Guilford
Warren	1786	Kent	Litchfield	Litchfield	1742	Hartford Woodbury New Haven
Washington	1779	Woodbury Litchfield Kent New Milford	Litchfield	Washington	1832	Litchfield Woodbury
Waterbury	1686	----	New Haven	Waterbury	1779	Woodbury
Waterford	1801	New London	New London	New London	original	----
Watertown	1780	Waterbury	Litchfield	Watertown	1834	Waterbury
Westbrook	1840	Saybrook	Middlesex	Westbrook	1854	Old Saybrook
West Hartford	1854	Hartford	Hartford	Hartford	original	----
West Haven	1921	Orange	New Haven	West Haven	1941	New Haven
Weston	1787	Fairfield	Fairfield	Westport	1835	Weston Fairfield Norwalk
(Weston, est. 1832 from Fairfield was annexed to Westport, 1875)						
Westport	1835	Fairfield Norwalk Weston	Fairfield	Westport	1835	Fairfield Norwalk Weston
Wethersfield	1634	----	Hartford	Newington	1975	Hartford

TOWN	TOWN EST.	PARENT TOWN	COUNTY	PROBATE DISTRICT	DATE EST.	PARENT DISTRICT
Willington	1727	-----	Tolland	Tolland	1830	Stafford
Wilton	1802	Norwalk	Fairfield	Norwalk	1802	Fairfield Stamford
Winchester	1771	-----	Litchfield	Winchester	1838	Norfolk
Windham	1692	-----	Windham	Windham	1719	Hartford New London
Windsor	1633	-----	Hartford	Windsor	1855	Hartford
Windsor Locks	1854	Windsor	Hartford	Windsor Locks	1961	Hartford
Wolcott	1796	Waterbury Southington	New Haven	Waterbury	1779	Woodbury
Woodbridge	1784	New Haven Milford	New Haven	New Haven	original	-----
Woodbury	1673	-----	Litchfield	Woodbury	1719	Hartford Fairfield New Haven
Woodstock	1690	-----	Windham	Woodstock	1831	Pomfret

(part of Massachusetts until 1749)

##

CEMETERY RECORDS

Among the excellent indexed resources for genealogists are Connecticut's cemetery records. As a W.P.A. project, Charles R. Hale directed the transcription of the tombstones in over 2,000 cemeteries. These records were then merged into one master index of individual names. The transcripts are located at the CONNECTICUT STATE LIBRARY in 59 typed volumes and several hundred file-card drawers. The collection is also available on microfilm at various libraries and Mormon Stakes, but not at the Connecticut State Library. The genealogist should also be aware of the many published cemetery records that have appeared in the "New England Historical and Genealogical Register," "Connecticut Ancestry," "Connecticut Nutmegger," and many other genealogical publications. Many local historical societies as well have transcribed local cemetery records.

##

CHURCH RECORDS

Under the direction of the Connecticut State Librarian George S. Godard, churches from around the state were encouraged to deposit their original records at the CONNECTICUT STATE LIBRARY. Many of these records have been microfilmed, and about 25%, mainly Congregational, have been indexed by names of individuals. (For Quaker records, see entry for Rhode Island Historical Society Library.)

##

MILITARY RECORDS

A good deal has been written about the military contributions of Connecticut, "The Provision State." There are printed lists of those who served from Connecticut in most wars dating from the colonial period along with numerous Civil War regimental histories.

IMMIGRATION AND NATURALIZATION RECORDS

Federal district court records are useful to the genealogist for immigration and naturalization papers. An immigrant could be naturalized in virtually any Connecticut court prior to the twentieth century. Some naturalization records and declarations of intention are still in the county courthouses, in the court files at the Connecticut State Library, or at the National Archives - Boston Branch in Waltham, Massachusetts. Under an agreement with the National Archives and Records Service, copies of records from the county courthouses (Superior Courts) and the State Library were transferred to Waltham in December 1984. Starting in 1906, Connecticut naturalization records were centralized and filed at the federal district courts in Hartford, New Haven, or Bridgeport. If the researcher has no idea where to go or what district court may contain his ancestor's naturalization papers, he should seek assistance from his nearest office of immigration and naturalization.

****

NEWSPAPERS

Charles R. Hale compiled abstracts of marriage and death notices reported in Connecticut newspapers from 1755 to about 1870, and a statewide index to the abstracts. This material is available at the Connecticut State Library and also on microfilm. A Preliminary Checklist of Connecticut Newspapers 1755-1975, prepared by the Connecticut State Library under the direction of Don Gustafson and published in two volumes, in 1978, is a useful guide to the state's newspapers and their repositories.

****

COURT RECORDS

Most civil and criminal court records for Connecticut, prior to about 1850, can be found at the CONNECTICUT STATE LIBRARY. Other material is in the Judicial District Superior Courts, geographical area courts, and town clerks' offices. Records at the State Library are described in Records of the Judicial Department (Part A): Court Records in the Connecticut State Library, 1636-1945 (1977; out of print). A 1985-86 survey, based at the State Library, will compile a database of and revised guide to historical court records across the state.

****

LIBRARIES

There are public libraries in every town in Connecticut. Their holdings vary greatly. The majority of them have small collections which may include items of genealogical interest. Many are open 12 hours a week or less and do not have staff to do any research. For a list of all libraries, consult the American Library Directory in most large libraries to see what is available and what hours of service are offered.

BRIDGEPORT - <u>BRIDGEPORT PUBLIC LIBRARY</u>
925 Broad Street
Bridgeport, CT 06604
203-576-7417
Mon-Thurs 9-9, Fri/Sat 9-5
(closed Sat. in summer)

I-95 exit 27 (Lafayette Street)
Right to State St., right to
Broad St. Parking at Cross-
roads Mall.

Photocopying $.15. By mail $.15 per page with $5 minimum charge. Microfilm
reader and reader/printer $.25; by mail $.30 with $5 minimum charge. Basic
holdings: Bridgeport; Connecticut; and New England. Microfilmed U.S. census
for Connecticut, 1800-1910. Obituary index for Bridgeport area, 1978-83.
Cemetery records (Hale collection for Bridgeport, Fairfield, and Stratford).
Papers of area genealogists and S.A.R. branch. Complete Bridgeport city
directories (1855-date) and most city directories for Connecticut cities (circa
1935-date). Newspapers (on microfilm, 1861-date). Soon to acquire Barbour
collection of vital records on microfilm. Coats of arms card index. Boston
Transcript and other microcards. American Genealogical-Biographical Index. DAR
lineage books. Periodicals. Maps and atlases. Strong collection.

BRIDGEPORT - <u>DEPARTMENT OF ARCHIVES, RECORDS AND INFORMATION SERVICES</u>
City of Bridgeport
Room 14, City Hall, 45 Lyon
  Terrace
Bridgeport, CT 06604
203-576-8192
Mon-Fri 9-5 (subject to change)

I-95 to exit 27A (Routes 8-25),
take first exit (Golden Hill
Street). Continue through first
onto Golden Hill St., first left
is Lyon Terrace. Room 14 is on
basement level of City Hall.

Collection of city government records. Includes voter registration cards and
lists, 1822-1963; tax assessment lists, 1821-22, 1866, c. 1890-c.1963; and
building permit applications, 1889-c.1960.

FAIRFIELD - <u>FAIRFIELD HISTORICAL SOCIETY LIBRARY</u>
636 Old Post Road
Fairfield, CT 06430
203-259-1598
Mon-Fri 9:30-4:30, Sunday 1-5

From I-95 take Exit 22. Turn
left & go to Rte 1. Turn right
for 1 block. Turn left onto Beach
Rd. After 1 block, turn right
onto Old Post Road. FHS is 2nd
building on left.

Open to public. Fee for preliminary research $3/query. Photocopying $.25/page
of copy plus $.75 for postage & handling. Books do not circulate. No interli-
brary loan. Holdings: Local histories, sermons, monographs, genealogies, bio-
graphies, maps, manuscripts, photographs, local and Fairfield County genealogical and biographical reference works, collections of genealogical and shipping
research working papers, almanacs, city directories, church, cemetery, court,
school and tax records, diaries.

HARTFORD - <u>CONNECTICUT HISTORICAL SOCIETY LIBRARY</u>

1 Elizabeth Street
Hartford, CT 06105
203-236-5621
Mon-Sat 9-5
(Closed Sat. Mem Day-Labor Day)

From Rte 84, exit 46 (Sisson St).
Turn right at end of ramp. At
Farmington Ave. (traffic light)
turn left. Right on Girard Ave.
Elizabeth St. second intersection.
Turn right. Parking lot second
drive on right.

Facilities: Patrons may bring own lunch and eat in docent lounge or on grounds. Restaurants 5 blocks away. Photocopying available $.15. (By mail $.25 per page). Two microfilm readers, one reader/printer. Microfiche reader. No Interlibrary Loan except for duplicate reels of Hartford Courant. Members may borrow duplicate town histories and genealogies for one month. Charge: $2 per volume (limit - 3 volumes). Staff genealogist or genealogical volunteer will conduct a search of indexed collections, within limits, for a specific name or two. Holdings: Connecticut histories, monographs, almanacs, city directories, sermons, biographies, Americana; genealogical reference works, Connecticut censuses and indexes in print to New England Federal census records; copies of church, town, and public records grouped by town and genealogical manuscript data grouped by family; historical manuscripts - personal correspondence, diaries, account books, newspapers and photographs.

HARTFORD - <u>CONNECTICUT STATE LIBRARY</u> (see entry on page 5)

MANCHESTER - <u>THE CHURCH OF JESUS CHRIST OF LATTER DAY SAINTS - HARTFORD STAKE BRANCH GENEALOGICAL LIBRARY</u>

30 Woodside Street
Manchester, CT 06040
203-649-6547
Tues 10-2, Wed/Thur 7PM-9PM
  Fri 10-2, Sat 9-5
Mailing address: P.O. Box 500
  Ellington, CT 06029

Rte 84/86-Silver Lane exit. Go right. At stop light turn left toward Manchester. At town line, the street changes to Spencer St. Continue to shopping center. Take right (Hillstown Rd.) Woodside is first right at stop sign.

8 microfilm readers, 6 microfiche readers. No interlibrary loan. Small collection of books. Copy of the card catalog of the main library in Salt Lake City, Utah on microfilm and the supplement and eventual replacement for it which is on microfiche called the Genealogical Library Catalog. <u>The International Genealogical Index</u> which consists of 82 million entries of births or christenings and marriages world wide. The microfiche <u>Family Registry</u>, a tool to coordinate research among people working on the same lines. The Accelerated Indexing Systems microfiche collection of heads of household from many census, tax lists and other records. Contains names from 1790-1850 and more recent listings in the West. Access to the millions of rolls of microfilm that contain original records from around the world.

MIDDLETOWN - <u>GODFREY MEMORIAL LIBRARY</u>

134 Newfield Street   Rte 91 to Rte 66 (exit 18). Go
Middletown, CT 06457   6 1/2 miles to Wesleyan University
203-346-4375   Turn left onto Newfield Street,
Mon-Fri 9-4   which is Rte 72 north.

Photocopier $.25, microfilm reader and microfiche reader. Will answer brief questions by mail. No Interlibrary Loan. Basic holdings: Local history and genealogy collections. Coverage mostly New England, but some for the rest of the United States as well. Publication: <u>The American Genealogical and Biographical Index</u>.

NEW CANAAN - <u>THE CHURCH OF JESUS CHRIST OF LATTER-DAY SAINTS YORKTOWN STAKE BRANCH GENEALOGICAL LIBRARY</u>

682 South Avenue   One mile north of Merritt Parkway
New Canaan, CT 06840   (I-15). Exit 37. At the church's
203-966-9511   meetinghouse on South Avenue
(hours to be announced)   across from Waveny Park.

Three microfilm readers. No Interlibrary Loan. Collection the same as Mormon Library in Manchester. (see above)

NEW CANAAN - <u>NEW CANAAN HISTORICAL SOCIETY LIBRARY</u>

13 Oenoke Ridge   Merritt Parkway - Exit 37. North.
New Canaan, CT 06840   Go through town center. 4 blocks
203-966-1776   north of center.
Tues-Sat 9:30-12:30, 2-4

One photocopier, microfilm reader. Strong collection covering New Canaan, Fairfield County and New England.

NEW HAVEN - <u>NEW HAVEN COLONY HISTORICAL SOCIETY. WHITNEY LIBRARY</u>

114 Whitney Avenue   Rte 91, exit 4 (Trumbull St. exit)
New Haven, CT 06510   At 2nd stop light turn right onto
203-562-4183   Whitney Ave. Parking on south
Tues-Fri, 10-4:45   side of building.

Fee: $2 per day for non-members. Research fee $10 per hour. Microfilm/fiche reader/printer. Photocopying $.45. No Interlibrary Loan. Holdings: Printed books, pamphlets, broadsides, maps, manuscripts, microforms and pictorial records of New Haven history from 1638 to date, including genealogical reference works, family histories, vital records, city directories, church and cemetery records, New Haven city and county documents (1638-1901), New Haven County Superior Court documents (1789-1905), military collections, school records, harbor and maritime collections, political papers, records of benevolent societies, correctional institutions, local business, C of C, military, census, and probate records on microfilm, some ethnic material including an Afro-American collection.

STAMFORD - <u>FERGUSON LIBRARY</u>
            One Public Library Plaza   Corner of Bedford and Broad Sts.
            Stamford, CT 06904   Take Merritt Parkway Exit 35 and
            203-964-1000   Connecticut Turnpike exit 7. Muni-
            Mon-Fri 9-9, Sat 9-5:30   cipal parking lot one block from
             Sun 1-5 (Sept-May)   library.

Photocopiers, $.10 per page, microfilm readers, reader/printers, $.15 per page.
Interlibrary Loan honored. Collection: Strong Local History and Genealogical
Collection.   Strong on Connecticut materials and for Westchester County, N.Y.,
and for New England.

                    ****

SOCIETIES

<u>CONNECTICUT HISTORICAL SOCIETY</u>
1 Elizabeth Street
Hartford, CT 06105
203-236-5621

Founded 1825. Dues: $15 per person out-of-state, $20 per person in-state.
Meetings: Monthly, first Tues. of each month except Summer. In the Auditorium
of the Connecticut Historical Society. Publications: CHS scholarly <u>Bulletin</u>,
and <u>Notes</u> <u>and</u> <u>News</u> newsletter, are both issued quarterly, and are free with
membership. Submissions for the <u>Bulletin</u> must be typed, double-spaced, with
correct bibliographical citations. First issue, November, 1934. (For Library:
see entry under CONNECTICUT - LIBRARIES)

                    _____

<u>CONNECTICUT SOCIETY OF GENEALOGISTS</u>
P.O. Box 435
Glastonbury, CT 06033
203-633-4203

Founded in 1968. Dues: $22 per family or individual. Meetings: Seven regular
meetings on the third Saturday of the month from Sept to May except December, at
various locations around the state. Publications: "Connecticut Nutmegger."
Subscription $10 (or free with membership). Queries accepted for members only.
Each member may submit 3 queries per month. Journal's first issue 1968. Available from CSG office. Reprints made of all volumes. Ancestry Volumes 1-5
(covering surnames beginning with A through Ha).

                    _____

NEW HAVEN COLONY HISTORICAL SOCIETY (See entry under CONNECTICUT - LIBRARIES)

Founded: 1862. Dues: Individual membership $20, family $35, library $15.
Meetings: Sept-May monthly membership, exhibit openings, lunch-time lectures,
courses and workshops (including genealogy). Publications: Historical
monographs, and family genealogies, Papers, v. 1-10, Journal, March 1952 - (v.
1-16 indexed), irregular newsletters and special announcements.

LOCAL HISTORY AND GENEALOGY: A SUBSECTION OF THE CONNECTICUT LIBRARY
ASSOCIATION
C/O Elizabeth Abbe, Chairperson
Connecticut Historical Society
1 Elizabeth Street
Hartford, CT 06105

Founded 1980: to provide a specific forum of communication for librarians,
teachers, researchers and curators who are interested in and/or responsible for
Connecticut local history and genealogy resources and education, and to endeavor
to improve repository collection methods and reference service.

Dues: $3 per year. Meetings: 4 times/year between Hartford and New Haven.

POLISH GENEALOGICAL SOCIETY OF CONNECTICUT
8 Lyle Road   Pres: Jonathan D. Shea
New Britain, CT 06053

Started 1984 as an outgrowth of an adult education course in Polish-American
history. Dues: $7 annual. May go up in 1986. Projects: cemetery inscription
program; obituary file. Biannual publication in progress.

STAMFORD GENEALOGICAL SOCIETY, INC.
P.O. Box 249
Stamford, CT 06904

Founded 1954 "to promote and assist in genealogical research." Dues: $10
Meetings: Sept to May at various locations. Quarterly publication: "Connecticut Ancestry" (formerly "Bulletin of the Stamford Genealogical Society"). First
issue, 1958 - Name changed in Nov 1971. Back issues available from the society.

****

BOOKS AND ARTICLES

Abbe, Elizabeth. "Connecticut Genealogical Research: Sources and Suggestions" The New England Historical and Genealogical Register, 134 (1980), 3-26, and in Genealogical Research in New England, Genealogical Publishing Co., 1984.

Kemp, Thomas Jay. Connecticut Researcher's Handbook. Detroit: Gale Research, Inc., 1982.

Shnare, Robert E., Jr. Local Historical Resources in Connecticut: A Guide to Their Use. Darien: The Connecticut League of Historical Societies, Inc., 1975.

Sperry, Kip. Connecticut Sources for Family Historians and Genealogists. Logan, Utah: Everton Publishers. 1980.

Wright, Norman Edgar. Genealogy in America. (Vol. 1, Massachusetts, Connecticut, and Maine). Salt Lake City: Deseret Book Co., 1968.

****

MAINE

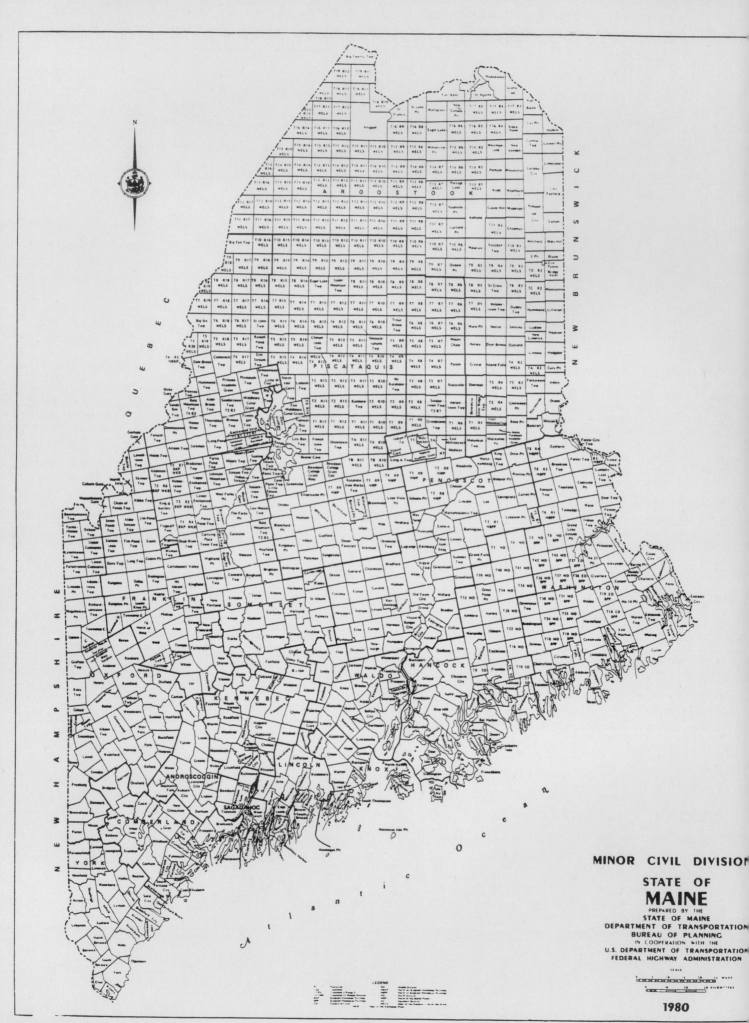

MINOR CIVIL DIVISION

STATE OF
MAINE

PREPARED BY THE
STATE OF MAINE
DEPARTMENT OF TRANSPORTATION
BUREAU OF PLANNING
IN COOPERATION WITH THE
U.S. DEPARTMENT OF TRANSPORTATION
FEDERAL HIGHWAY ADMINISTRATION

1980

MAINE

Maine was part of Massachusetts until 1820 and the mandatory recording of vital records began in 1892. Since the state is so large, it is wise to concentrate search efforts on centers with collections and facilities. The major repositories of genealogical collections in Maine are The Maine Historical Society Library in Portland, and the Maine State Archives and the Maine State Library in Augusta. The latter two agencies share the same building. Maine census indexes and microfilm from 1790 to 1850 are available at these locations, and they also have published town records, histories and genealogies.

Deeds and probate records in Maine are located at County Courthouses. (See the list following.) York County encompassed all of Maine until 1760. York Deeds through 1737 are in published form, as are Maine Wills 1640-1760. Both are in major genealogical libraries in Maine and Massachusetts.

****

VITAL RECORDS TO 1892

MAINE STATE ARCHIVES
State House Station 84
Augusta, ME 04333
Mon-Fri 8:30-4:00
207-289-2451

From Maine Turnpike exit 202-Augusta. At rotary, bear right onto Rte 27 (State St.). Past capitol. 1st driveway. Archives and library on left.

Registration required. Open to general public. Photocopying service: $.25 for xerox and $.50 for reader/printer and other reproduction services available upon request. 13 microfilm readers and 2 reader/printers. Limited service by mail. Holdings: Non-current state and municipal records. Superior and Supreme Judicial Court Records prior to 1930 (except Lincoln County which is available at MSA on microfilm only. Originals still at Wiscasset). Military Records of the Office of the Adjutant General for the Civil War (and some transcripts from Mass. Archives for the War of 1812). Records of the Maine Land Office. County Marriages returns for the various Maine Counties (except Cumberland, Lincoln, Oxford, and Franklin). The Graves Registration Index for veterans of the Revolutionary through Spanish American Wars. Original census returns for 1850 through 1880 with additional social statistics, agricultural, and industrial schedules 1850 through 1870. Many microfilms of the town records (vital statistics and town meetings) are described in the Microfilm list (partially reproduced in this publication): Maine Town and Census Records (now priced $1) and Public Record Repositories ($5.25). Besides the census records and the microfilms of the town and city vital records, are the microfilms of the State Vital Statistics for the entire State in four time periods: 1892-1907, 1908-1922, 1923-1936, and 1937-1955. These additional microfilm sources are available from self-service file cabinets. Brides Index 1895-1953; Soundex to the 1880 and 1900 census, microfilm of all Maine Census (except 1890 but the Civil War returns do survive) from 1790 to 1910. The 1798 direct tax of Maine (NEHGS publication). Divorce index 1892-1964 (most recent addition to microfilm). Land Office Plans (useful for tracing location of pioneers in unorganized townships). Deeds for several counties: Oxford (1800-1862 western and eastern registries), Somerset (1809-1861), Piscataquis (1838-1862), Knox (1836-1860, transcripts from Lincoln Co.), Kennebec Co. (1799-1872 but no index). Vital Records prior to 1892 (about 20 per-cent return). Ship Passenger Lists 1907-1919. Maine Federal Extension Records, 1915-1948. Board of Assessors Maps. Acts and Resolves 1820-1967. Probate for one county - Aroostook (1840-1900). Index to Somerset County Probate: from formation of county until the 1970s. Soldiers who died in WWII and Repatriation of War Dead.

VITAL RECORDS 1892 TO PRESENT

OFFICE OF VITAL STATISTICS   (Directions same as above)
DEPARTMENT OF HUMAN SERVICES
State House Station #11
Augusta, Maine 04330

Note: Original jurisdiction over Vital Records is with the cities and towns. If the town is known, it is possible to write to the city or town clerk for information. However, limited staffing in many smaller towns prevents a return answer in some cases.

###

This list of Maine Towns is taken from Public Records Repositories in Maine (Rev. Ed. 9/24/76). Augusta: Maine State Archives. For a more detailed summary, consult the publication mentioned. Many Maine town records have been partially destroyed by fire and this is indicated by code. Codes used are F which indicates some loss by fire within the dates given, therefore records are not complete. Ind indicates the records are indexed and therefore would probably be checked for individual names by the town clerk. MSA means microfilm copy at the Maine State Archives. Inc means incomplete.

TOWN	COUNTY	ORGANIZED	TOWN RECORDS	VITAL RECORDS	CODES
Abbot	Piscataquis	31 Jan 1827	1900-	1900	F
Acton	York	6 Mar 1830		1830-1892	MSA/Inc
				1892-	Ind
Adams (see Crawford)					
Addison	Washington	14 Feb 1797	1824-	1834	F/Ind
				1853-1871	MSA
Albion	Kennebec	9 Mar 1804	1700s-	1700s-	
(Fairfax 1804, Ligonia 1821, Albion 1824)				1802-1891	MSA
Alexander	Washington	19 Jan 1825	1975-	1975-	F
				1784-1926	MSA
Alfred	York	25 Feb 1808	1724-	1890	F/Ind
				1803-1892	MSA
Allagash Plan-tation	Aroostook	14 June 1886	1892-	1892-	F/Ind
Alno	Lincoln	25 Jun 1794	1855-	1892-	F
(New Milford 1794, Alna 1811)			1795-1891	1795-1891	MSA
Alton	Penobscot	9 Mar 1844	1800s-	1894-	F/Ind
				1859-1940	MSA
Amherst	Hancock	5 Feb 1831	1850-	1856-	F/Inc
				1783-1891	MSA

TOWN	COUNTY	ORGANIZED	TOWN RECORDS	VITAL RECORDS	CODES
Amity	Aroostook	19 Mar 1836	1960-	1893	F
				1862-1882	MSA
Andover	Oxford	23 Jun 1804	1800s-	1800s-	Inc
(East Andover 1804, Andover 1820)				1795-1891	MSA
Anson	Somerset	1 Mar 1798	1899-1913; 1931-	1882-	F
			1798-1855	1798-1890	MSA
Appleton	Knox	28 Jan 1829	1820-	1700s-	Inc/Ind
				1774-1892	MSA
Arrowsic	Sagadahoc	2 Mar 1841	1892-	1860-	
				1741-1891	MSA
Arundel	York	1 Apr 1915	1916-	1916-	Ind
(N. Kennebunkport 1915, Arundel 1957)			1678-1892	1678-1892	MSA
(see also Kennebunkport)					
Ashland	Aroostook	18 Feb 1862		1863-	Ind
(Dalton from 1869-1876)					
Athens	Somerset	7 Mar 1804	1900-	1900-	F/Ind
Atkinson	Piscataquis	12 Feb 1819	1888-	1900-	Inc
				1766-1901	MSA
Auburn	Androscoggin	24 Feb 1842	1840-	1700s-	Ind
				1751-1954	MSA
Augusta	Kennebec	20 Feb 1797	1900-	1930-	Inc
(Harrington from 20 Feb to 9 June 1797)				1780-1896	MSA/Inc
Aurora	Hancock	1 Feb 1831		1945-	F
(Hampton until 6 Feb 1833)					
Avon	Franklin	22 Feb 1802	1917-	1892-	F
				1766-1850	MSA
Baileyville	Washington	19 Feb 1828		1861-1939	MSA
Baldwin	Cumberland	23 June 1802	1790s-	1790s-	
			1802-1846	1802-1892	MSA
Bancroft	Aroostook	21 Feb 1878	1910-	1892-	
Bangor	Penobscot	25 Feb 1791	1812-	1800-	Ind
				1775-1892	MSA/Inc
Bar Harbor	Hancock	23 Feb 1796	1892-	1892-	F/Ind
(Eden until 25 Mar 1913)			1798-1884	1796-1848	MSA
Baring Plantation	Washington	19 Jan 1825	1892-1931	1892-1931; 1941-	Ind
Barnard Plantation	Piscataquis	20 Mar 1834	1921-	1921-	F
Bath	Sagadahoc	17 Feb 1781	1753-	1892-	Ind
				1757-1892	MSA
Beals	Washington	7 Apr 1925	1925-	1925-	
Beaver Cove Plantation	Piscataquis	17 Mar 1975	1975-	1975-	
Beddington	Washington	31 Jan 1833	1844-	1882-	Ind
				1792-1892	MSA
Belfast	Waldo	29 Jun 1773	1853-	1892-	Ind
			1773-1903	1773-1903	MSA
Belgrade	Kennebec	3 Feb 1796	1906-	1700s-	F
				1758-1892	MSA
Belmont	Waldo	5 Feb 1814	1800s-	1892-	F/Ind
				1855-1883	MSA
Benedicta	Aroostook	1 Feb 1873	1949-	1928-	F

MAINE

TOWN	COUNTY	ORGANIZED	TOWN RECORDS	VITAL RECORDS	CODES
Benton	Kennebec	16 Mar 1842		1892-	Ind
(Sebasticook until 19 Jun 1850)				1841-1891	MSA
Berwick	York	9 Jun 1713	1700-	1700-	
			1701-1892	1701-1892	MSA
Bethel	Oxford	10 Jun 1796	1796-	1867-	Ind
				1745-1923	MSA
Biddeford	York	17 Nov 1718	1872-	1872-	F/Ind
			1653-1786	1653-1923	MSA
Bingham	Somerset	6 Feb 1812	1812-	1812-	Ind
				1759-1891	MSA
Blaine	Aroostook	10 Feb 1874	1942-	1892-	F
Blanchard Plantation	Piscataquis	17 Mar 1831	1800s-	1800s-	F
			1831-1959		MSA
Blue Hill	Hancock	30 Jan 1789	1789-	1700-	Inc
				1785-1890;1892-1923	MSA
Boothbay	Lincoln	3 Nov 1764	1763-	1763-	Ind
				1796-1892	MSA
Boothbay Harbor	Lincoln	16 Feb 1889	1889-	1889-	
				1763-1891	MSA
Bowdoin	Sagadahoc	21 Mar 1788	1788-	1892-	F
				1763-1891	MSA
Bowdoinham	Sagadahoc	18 Sep 1762	1900-	1725-	F/Ind
				1776-1891	MSA
Bowerbank	Piscataquis	4 Mar 1839	1966-	1966-	
(earlier records at Town Hall. Permission needed to search)				1832-1932	MSA
Bradford	Penobscot	12 Mar 1831		1862-	Inc
			1819-1854	1863-1940	MSA
Bradley	Penobscot	3 Feb 1835	1770-	1770-	
				1805-1893	MSA
Bremen	Lincoln	19 Feb 1828	1828-	1828-	
				1756-1892	MSA
Brewer	Penobscot	22 Feb 1812	1812-	1770-	Ind
		Lineage books	1743-1859	1806-1943	MSA
Bridgewater	Aroostook	2 Mar 1858	1950s-	1894-	F/Ind
Bridgton	Cumberland	7 Feb 1794	1794-	1794-	Ind
				1785-1865	MSA
Brighton Plantation	Somerset	20 Jun 1816	1800s-	1892-	
(North Hill until 29 Jan 1827)			1816-1837	1840-1918	MSA
Bristol	Lincoln	21 Jun 1765	1765-	1892-	
			1765-1900	1765-1900	MSA
Brooklin	Hancock	9 Jun 1849	1849-	1849-	
(Port Watson until 23 Jul 1849)			1849-1898	1835-1936	MSA
Brooks	Waldo	10 Dec 1816	1930-	1892-	F
Brooksville	Hancock	13 Jun 1817	1966-	1817-	F
				1818-1940	MSA
Brownfield	Oxford	20 Feb 1802	1800s-	1802-	F
Brownville	Piscataquis	3 Feb 1824		1824-	Ind
				1812-1868	

TOWN	COUNTY	ORGANIZED	TOWN RECORDS	VITAL RECORDS	CODES
Brunswick	Cumberland	26 Jan 1739	1830s-	1830s-	Ind
			1735-1872	1735-1910	MSA
Buckfield	Oxford	16 Mar 1793	1797-	1782-	Ind
				1700-1891	MSA
Bucksport	Hancock	27 Jun 1792	1800-	1800-	
(Buckstown until 12 June 1817)				1775-1920	MSA
Buckstown (See Bucksport)					
Burlington	Penobscot	8 Mar 1832	1840-	1840-	
				1769-1891	MSA
Burnham	Waldo	4 Feb 1824	1824-	1892-	F/Ind
				1821-1891	MSA
Buxton	Oxford	14 Jul 1772	1740-	1790-	Ind
				1773-1890	MSA
Byron	Oxford	24 Jan 1833	1874-	1880-	
			1814-1892	1814-1892	MSA
Calais	Washington	16 Jun 1809	1809-	1890-	F/Ind
				1824-1911	MSA
Cambridge	Somerset	8 Feb 1834	1834-	1800-	Ind
				1792-1896	MSA
Camden	Knox	17 Feb 1791	1891-	1891-	Ind
(Divided into Camden & Rockport 1891)			1783-1892	1783-1892	MSA
Canaan	Somerset	18 Jun 1788	1880-	1700s-	F/Ind
				1776-1910	MSA
Canton	Oxford	5 Feb 1821	1818-1866; 1891-		F
Cape Elizabeth	Cumberland	1 Nov 1765	1903-	1903-	Ind
			1765-1876	1765-1891	MSA
Cape Porpoise (See Kennebunkport)					
Caratunk Plantation	Somerset	1840	1854-	1854-	
				1854-1904	MSA
Caribou	Aroostook	5 Apr 1859	1859-	1892-	
(Lyndon until 1877)			1848-1929	1848-1929	MSA
Carmel	Penobscot	21 Jun 1811	1964-	1850s-	F
				1760-1891	MSA
Carrabassett Valley	Franklin	23 Sep 1972	1972-		
Carroll Plantation	Penobscot	20 Mar 1845	1928-	1928-	F
Carthage	Franklin	20 Feb 1826	1826-	1828-	
				1812-1891	MSA
Cary Plantation	Aroostook	21 Feb 1878	1972-		F
				1862-1882	MSA
Casco	Cumberland	18 Mar 1841	1873-	1920-	F
				1841-1892	MSA
Castine	Hancock	10 Feb 1796	1796-	1800-	
			1796-1891	1796-1891	MSA
Castle Hill	Aroostook	25 Feb 1903	1940s-	1892-	Ind
				1855-1892	MSA
Caswell Plantation	Aroostook	14 Apr 1879	1945-	1898-	F
Centerville	Washington	16 Mar 1842		1800s-	F
				1770-1865	MSA

TOWN	COUNTY	ORGANIZED	TOWN RECORDS	VITAL RECORDS	CODES
Chandlerville (See Detroit)					
Chapman	Aroostook	14 Feb 1879		1868-	Ind
				1868-1891	MSA
Charleston	Penobscot	16 Feb 1811	1811-	1811-	Ind
			1809-1897	1809-1897	MSA
Charlotte	Washington	19 Jan 1825	1821-	1821-	Ind
				1816-1892	MSA
Chelsea	Kennebec	17 Aug 1850	1851-	1851-	Ind
				1782-1892	MSA
Cherryfield	Washington	9 Feb 1816	1842-	1845-	Inc
				1854-1939	MSA
Chester	Penobscot	26 Feb 1834	1862-	1835-	Inc
				1788-1943	MSA
Chesterville	Franklin	20 Feb 1802	1900-	1785-	
				1788-1907	MSA
China	Kennebec	8 Feb 1796	1797-	1892-	
(Harlem until 1818)			1785-1891	1785-1891	MSA
Clifton	Penobscot	7 Aug 1848	1860-	1892-	Ind
(Maine until 1849)				1848-1892	MSA
Clinton	Kennebec	28 Feb 1795	1892-	1892-	
				1797-1898	MSA
Codyville Plantation	Washington	14 Apr 1845	1922-	1892-	Inc
Columbia	Washington	8 Feb 1796	1796-	1892-	F/Ind
			1752-1860	1752-1860	MSA
Columbia Falls	Washington	25 Mar 1863	1796-	1860-	
				1863-1891	MSA
Cooper	Washington	6 Feb 1822	1907-	1892-	F
				1878-1930	MSA
Coplin Plantation	Franklin	5 Feb 1895		1895-	
Corinna	Penobscot	11 Dec 1816		1892-	Ind/Inc
				1797-1891	MSA
Corinth	Penobscot	21 Jun 1811	1811-40; 1865-	1811-40;1865	Ind
				1785-1895	MSA
Cornish	York	27 Feb 1794		1857-	F/Ind
Cornville	Somerset	24 Feb 1798	1794-	1794-	Ind
				1772-1891	MSA
Coxhall (See Lyman)					
Cranberry Isles	Hancock	16 Mar 1830	1830-	1830-	
				1783-1890	MSA
Crawford	Washington	11 Feb 1828	1901-	1890-	F
				1827-1900	MSA
Crystal	Aroostook	21 Mar 1901	1923-	1800s-	F/Ind
				1854-1896	MSA
Cumberland	Cumberland	19 Mar 1821	1821-	1700s-	Ind
				1720-1892	MSA
Cushing	Knox	30 Jan 1789	1845-	1818-	Ind
				1735-1920	MSA
Cutler	Washington	26 Jan 1826	1843-1849;1900-	1900-	F
				1844-1896	MSA
Cyr Plantation	Aroostook	12 Mar 1870	1892-	1892-	Ind

TOWN	COUNTY	ORGANIZED	TOWN RECORDS	VITAL RECORDS	CODES
Dallas Plantation	Franklin	25 Feb 1845	1921-	1892-	
Dalton (See Ashland)					
Damariscotta	Lincoln	26 July 1847	1864-	1892-	Ind
				1848-1891	MSA
Danforth	Washington	17 Mar 1860	1936-	1892-	Ind
				1860-1891	MSA
Dayton	York	7 Apr 1854	1854-	1854-	Ind
			1832-1899	1832-1899	MSA
Deblois	Washington	4 Mar 1852	1852-	1855-	
Dedham	Hancock	7 Feb 1837	1932-	1820-	Ind/Inc
				1787-1940	MSA
Deer Isle	Hancock	30 Jan 1789	1789-1853;1958	1786-	F
				1768-1940	MSA
Denmark	Oxford	20 Feb 1807	1807-	1807-	
Dennistown Plantation	Somerset	5 Mar 1895	1910-	1900-	
Trickey Family Records 1614-1938				1840-1940	MSA
Dennysville	Washington	13 Feb 1818	1818-	1818-	Ind
				1790-1917	MSA
Detroit (Chandlerville until 1841)	Somerset	18 Feb 1828	1816-	1802-	
			1780-1892	1780-1892	MSA
Dexter	Penobscot	17 Jun 1816	1816-	1802-	Ind/Inc
				1761-1897	MSA
Dickeyville (See Frenchville)					
Dixfield	Oxford	21 Jun 1803	1803-	1804-	Ind/Inc
			1803-1892	1803-1892	MSA
Dixmont	Penobscot	28 Feb 1807	1906-	1821-	Ind
				1800-1894	MSA
Dover-Foxcroft (Foxcroft 1812, Dover 1822, merged 1915)	Piscataquis	29 Feb 1812	1800s-	1800s-	
				1792-1894	MSA
Dresden	Lincoln	25 Jun 1794	1794-	1892-	Ind
			1771-1906	1771-1906	MSA
Drew Plantation	Penobscot	5 Apr 1921		1850s-	
				1853-1928	MSA
Durham	Androscoggin	17 Feb 1789	1961-	1774-1865;1892-	
				1744-1892	MSA
Dutton (See Glenburn)					
Dyer Brook	Aroostook	21 Mar 1891		1895-	Ind
E Plantation	Aroostook	26 Sep 1898	1966-		
Eagle Lake	Aroostook	12 Mar 1870	1890-	1892-	Inc
				1867-1950	MSA
East Livermore (See Livermore Falls)					
East Machias (Machisses from 1840-1841)	Washington	24 Jan 1826	1823-	1769-	Ind
				1709-1900	MSA
East Millinocket	Penobscot	21 Feb 1907	1907-	1907-	
East Thomaston (See Rockland)					
Eastbrook	Hancock	8 Feb 1837	1892-	1892-	
Easton	Aroostook	24 Feb 1865	1896-	1892-	Ind
Eastport	Washington	24 Feb 1798	1700s-	1700s-	F/Ind
				1778-1904	MSA

TOWN	COUNTY	ORGANIZED	TOWN RECORDS	VITAL RECORDS	CODES
Eddington	Penobscot	22 Feb 1811	1805-	1802-	F/Ind
				1802-1922	MSA
Eden (See Bar Harbor)					
Edgecomb	Lincoln	9 Mar 1774	1774-	1774-	Ind
			1774-1892	1774-1892	MSA
Edinburg	Penobscot	31 Jan 1835		1872-	F
				1835-1899	MSA
Eliot	York	1 Mar 1810	1810-	1892-	
			1810-1901	1810-1892	MSA
Elliotsville Plantation	Piscataquis	19 Feb 1835	1960-	1913-	
Ellsworth	Hancock	26 Feb 1800	1933-	1800s-	F/Ind
Embden	Somerset	22 Jun 1804	1820-	1892-	Inc
			1783-1892	1783-1892	MSA
Enfield	Penobscot	31 Jan 1835	1940-	1857-	F
Etna	Penobscot	15 Feb 1820	1900s-	1800s-	
				1742-1910	MSA
Eustis	Franklin	18 Feb 1871		1872-	
			Marriages	1871-1892	MSA
Exeter	Penobscot	16 Feb 1811	1950-	1950-	F
			1808-1893	1808-1893	MSA
Fairfax (See Albion)					
Fairfield	Somerset	18 Jun 1788	1788-	1788-	F/Ind
				1788-1867	MSA
Falmouth	Cumberland	12 Nov 1718	1718-1773;1850-	1712-	Inc
			1718-1773	1718-1773;1784-1892	MSA
Farmingdale	Kennebec	3 Apr 1852	1852-	1855-	Ind
				1852-1891	MSA
Farmington	Franklin	1 Feb 1794	1794-	1792-	Ind
				1741-1891	
Fayette	Kennebec	28 Feb 1795	1795-	1892-	F/Ind
				1785-1952	MSA
Forks Plantation	Somerset	20 Mar 1895		1800s-	
Fort Fairfield	Aroostook	11 Mar 1858	1858-	1892-	Ind
				1847-1892	MSA
Fort Kent	Aroostook	23 Feb 1869	1900-	1892-	Ind
Fox Isle (See North Haven)					
Foxcroft (See Dover-Foxcroft)					
Frankfort	Waldo	25 Jun 1789	1934-	1903-	F/Ind
Franklin	Hancock	24 Jan 1825	1813-	1813-	Ind
Freedom	Waldo	11 Jun 1813	1813-	1834-	Ind
				1777-1892	MSA
Freeport	Cumberland	14 Feb 1789	1789-	1789-	Ind
				1795-1892	MSA
Frenchville	Aroostook	23 Feb 1869	1900s-	1880-	F/Ind
(Dickeyville until 1871)			1869-1892	1869-1892	MSA
Friendship	Knox	25 Feb 1807	1824-	1824-	F/Ind
				1769-1889	MSA
Fryeburg	Oxford	11 Jan 1777	1773-	1777-	Ind
			1777-1892	1777-1892	MSA
Gardiner	Kennebec	17 Feb 1803		1892-	Ind
				1800-1891	MSA

TOWN	COUNTY	ORGANIZED	TOWN RECORDS	VITAL RECORDS	CODES
Garfield Plantation	Aroostook	5 Mar 1895	1958-	1892-	
Garland	Penobscot	16 Feb 1811	1936-	1859-	F/Ind
				1854-1950	MSA
Georgetown	Sagadahoc	13 Jun 1716	1716-	1750-	Ind
			1757-1940	1757-1940	MSA
Gilead	Oxford	23 Jun 1804	1800s-	1700s-	Ind
				1757-1892	MSA
Glenburn	Penobscot	29 Jan 1822	1822-	1892	F
				1800-1888	MSA
Glenwood Plantation	Aroostook	14 Feb 1867	1866-	1866-	F
Gorham	Cumberland	30 Oct 1764	1807-	1750-	F/Ind
			1733-1879	1721-1880	MSA/Inc
Gouldsboro	Hancock	16 Feb 1789	1789-	1792-	F
			1772-1898	1772-1898	MSA
Grand Falls Plantation	Penobscot	16 Nov 1878			
Grand Isle	Aroostook	2 Mar 1869	1869-	1892-	Ind
Grand Lake Stream Plantation	Washington	11 Feb 1897			
Gray	Cumberland	19 Jun 1778	1778-	1700s-	F/Ind
Great Pond Plantation	Hancock	5 Mar 1895	1950-	1894-	Ind
Greenbush	Penobscot	28 Feb 1834		1910-	Ind
				1774-1931	MSA
Greene	Androscoggin	18 Jun 1788	1788-	1788-	
				1748-1891	MSA
Greenfield	Penobscot	29 Jan 1834	1848-	1850s-	F/Ind
Greenville	Piscataquis	6 Feb 1836	1831-	1883-	
				1820-1892	MSA
Greenwood	Oxford	2 Feb 1816	1898-	1816-	F
			1813-1920	1797-1926	MSA
Guilford	Piscataquis	8 Feb 1816	1816-	1892-	Ind
				1770-1932	MSA
Hallowell	Kennebec	26 Apr 1771		1700s-	
			1761-1812	1761-1812	MSA
Hamlin	Aroostook	12 Mar 1870		1892-	
Hammond Plantation	Aroostook	17 Feb 1886	1885-	1885-	
				1864-1954	MSA
Hampden	Penobscot	24 Feb 1794	1794-	1892-	Inc/F
Hampton (See Aurora)					
Hancock	Hancock	21 Feb 1828	1917-	1890-	Ind
			1828-1891	1828-1891	MSA
Hanover	Oxford	14 Feb 1843		1791-	
				1807-1892	MSA
Harlem (See China)					
Harmony	Somerset	15 Jun 1803	1804-	1800-1850;1890-	
			1764-1864	1764-1864	MSA
Harpswell	Cumberland	25 Jan 1758	1900s-	1740s-	
				1769-1892	MSA

TOWN	COUNTY	ORGANIZED	TOWN RECORDS	VITAL RECORDS	CODES
Harrington	Washington	17 Jun 1797	1837-	1771-	F/Ind
	(See also Augusta)		delayed births	1851-1892	MSA
Harrison	Cumberland	8 Mar 1805	1820s-	1806-	F/Inc
			1805-1919	1805-1919	MSA
Hartford	Oxford	13 Jun 1798	1798-	1892-	
				1800-1891	MSA
Hartland	Somerset	7 Feb 1820	1820-	1894-	Ind/F
				1772-1891	MSA
Haynesville	Aroostook	18 Feb 1876		1892-	
Hebron	Oxford	6 Mar 1792	1792-	1792-	
			1700-1893	1700-1893	MSA
Hermon	Penobscot	13 Jun 1816		1930-	F
			Marriages	1872-1891	MSA
Hersey	Aroostook	25 Jan 1873	1873-	1890-	
			1862-1914	1862-1914	MSA
Highland Plantation	Somerset	18 Feb 1871	1972-	1972-	F
Hiram	Oxford	14 Jun 1814	1804-	1892-	
			Marriages	1815-1864	MSA
Hodgdon	Aroostook	11 Feb 1832	1950-	1800s-	Ind
				1837-1940	MSA
Holden	Penobscot	13 Apr 1852	1852-	1852-	
				1756-1945	MSA
Hollis	York	27 Feb 1798	1798-	1892-	Inc
			1781-1892	1781-1892	MSA
Hope	Knox	23 Jun 1804		1740-	
				1795-1925	MSA
Houlton	Aroostook	8 Mar 1831	1923-	1892-	F/Inc
Howard	(See Willimantic)				
Howland	Penobscot	10 Feb 1826	1911-	1892-	Ind/Inc
			births, deaths	1798-1937	MSA
Hudson	Penobscot	25 Feb 1825	1887-	1856-	Ind/Inc
				1856-1892	MSA
Huntressville	(See Lowell)				
Indian Island	Penobscot		1940s-	1962-	F
Indian Township	Washington			1970-	
Industry	Franklin	20 Jun 1803	1803-	1892-	Ind
				1738-1891	MSA
Island Falls	Aroostook	27 Feb 1872	1910	1910-	F
Islandport	(See Long Island Plantation)				
Isle Au Haut	Knox	28 Feb 1874	1951-	1875-	F
Islesboro	Waldo	30 Jan 1789	1789-	1789-	
Jackman	Somerset	5 Mar 1895	1883-	1892-	
Jackson	Waldo	12 Jun 1818	1818-	1809-	F/Inc
Jay	Franklin	26 Feb 1795	1865-	1700s-	Ind
			1779-1891	1779-1891	MSA
Jefferson	Lincoln	24 Feb 1807	1960s-	1770s-	
			1757-1891	1757-1891	MSA
Jonesboro	Washington	4 Mar 1809	1918-	1892-	Ind/F
				1766-1890	MSA
Jonesport	Washington	3 Feb 1832	1854-	1872-	Ind/F

TOWN	COUNTY	ORGANIZED	TOWN RECORDS	VITAL RECORDS	CODES
Joy (see Troy)					
Kenduskeag	Penobscot	20 Feb 1852	1852-	1852-	
				1852-1891	MSA
Kennebec (see Manchester)					
Kennebunk	York	24 Jun 1820	1850-	1739-	Ind
				1729-1892	MSA
Kennebunkport	York	5 Jul 1653	1837-	1856-	Ind
			1678-1892	1678-1892	MSA
Kilmarnock (see Medford)					
Kingfield	Franklin	24 Jan 1816	1816-	1892-	Ind
			1816-1862	1816-1862	MSA
Kingsbury					
Plantation	Piscataquis	22 Mar 1836	1892-	1892-	F
			1836-1868	1836-1868	MSA
Kingville (see Troy)					
Kirkland (see Hudson)					
Kittery	York	20 Nov 1652	1800s-		Ind
			1648-1896	1674-1892	MSA
Knox	Knox	12 Feb 1819	1820-	1700s-	Inc/Ind
				1777-1896	MSA
Lagrange	Penobscot	11 Feb 1832	1832-	1892-	
				1833-1891	MSA
Lake View					
Plantation	Piscataquis	16 Jun 1892	1905-	1892-	
Lakeville					
Plantation	Penobscot	29 Feb 1868	1940-	1880-	Inc
				1862-1955	MSA
Lamoine	Hancock	11 Feb 1870	1870-	1890-	
				1849-1935	MSA
Lebanon	York	17 Jun 1767	1969-	1892-	
			1765-1898	1765-1898	MSA
Lee	Penobscot	3 Feb 1832	1900-	1870-	F
			1780-1945	1780-1945	MSA
Leeds	Androscoggin	16 Feb 1801	1801-	1801-	
				1785-1891	MSA
Levand	Penobscot	14 Jun 1813	1920-	1872-	
				1769-1917	
Lewiston	Androscoggin	18 Feb 1795	1795-	1830-	
			1801-1839	1750-1900	MSA
Liberty	Waldo	31 Jan 1827	1856-	1856-	Ind
				1864-1891	MSA
Ligonier (see Albion)					
Limerick	York	6 Mar 1787			Inc
Limestone	Aroostook	26 Feb 1869	1861-	1892-	F
			Births	1862-1935	MSA
Limington	York	9 Feb 1792	1792-	1800-	Ind
			1792-1898	1792-1892	MSA
Lincoln	Penobscot	30 Jan 1829	1829-	1856-	Ind
			Index to	1829-1892	MSA
Lincoln					
Plantation	Oxford	15 Sep 1875	1875-	1890s-	

TOWN	COUNTY	ORGANIZED	TOWN RECORDS	VITAL RECORDS	CODES
Lincolnville	Waldo	23 Jun 1802	1802-	1802-	Ind/F
				1786-1892	
Linneus	Aroostook	19 Mar 1836		1840-	
			1840-1892	1784-1892	MSA
Lisbon	Androscoggin	22 Jun 1799	1799-	1782-	Ind/F
				1782-1893	MSA
Litchfield	Kennebec	18 Feb 1795	1922-	1700s-	Ind
			1785-1952	1785-1952	MSA
Littleton	Aroostook	18 Mar 1856		1892-	Ind
Livermore	Androscoggin	28 Feb 1795	1795-	1795-	
				1762-1891	MSA
Livermore Falls	Androscoggin	20 Mar 1843	1844-	1892-	Ind
Long Island Plantation	Hancock	11 Feb 1857	1900-	1900-	F
Lovell	Oxford	15 Nov 1800	1800-	1800-	Ind
				1785-1892	MSA
Lowell	Penobscot	9 Feb 1837	1900-	1892-	Ind/F
				1854-1939	
Lubec	Washington	21 Jun 1811	1820-	1820-	Ind
				1819-1892	MSA
Ludlow	Aroostook	21 Mar 1864	1840-	1840-	
Lyman	York	11 Mar 1778	1780-	1780-	F
			1850-1892	1850-1892	MSA
Lyndon (see Caribou)					
Machias	Washington	23 Jun 1784	1931-	1790-	Ind
			1773-1891	1773-1892	MSA
Machiasport	Washington	26 Jan 1826	1966-	1892-	F
				1859-1891	
Machisses (see East Machias)					
Macwahoc Plantation	Aroostook	16 Dec 1851	1850-	1892-	F
			1851-1896	1851-1896	MSA
Madawaska	Aroostook	24 Feb 1869	1869-	1871-	Ind
Madison	Somerset	7 Mar 1804	1892-	1892-	F
			Marriages	1939-1956	
Madrid	Franklin	29 Jan 1836	1956-	1892-	F
				1789-1891	MSA
Magalloway Plantation	Oxford	1883	1952-	1952-	F
Maine (see Clifton)					
Manchester	Kennebec	12 Aug 1850	1850-	1850-	
				1808-1908	MSA
Mansel (see Tremont)					
Mapleton	Aroostook	21 Feb 1878		1892-	
				1864-1891	MSA
Mariaville	Hancock	29 Feb 1836	1836-	1875-	Ind
Marshfield	Washington	30 Jun 1846	1846-	1700s-	
				1821-1892	MSA
Mars Hill	Aroostook	21 Feb 1867	1880s-	1900s-	
				1786-1892	MSA
Masardis	Aroostook	21 Mar 1839	1930-	1818-	Ind/F

TOWN	COUNTY	ORGANIZED	TOWN RECORDS	VITAL RECORDS	CODES
Matinicus Isle Plantation	Knox	22 Oct 1840	1889-	1891-	
			1840-1899	1840-1899	MSA
Mattawamkeag	Penobscot	14 Feb 1860	1860-	1865-	Ind
				1860-1891	MSA
Maxfield	Penobscot	6 Feb 1824	1962-	1971-	Ind/F
			1825-1891	1825-1891	MSA
Mechanic Falls	Androscoggin	22 Mar 1893	1893-	1893-	
Meddybemps	Washington	20 Feb 1841	1946-	1936-	Ind/F
Medford	Piscataquis	31 Jan 1824		1844-	F
			Marriage Intentions	1844-1891	MSA
Medway	Penobscot	8 Feb 1875	1875-	1850s-	
			Marriage Intentions	1856-1940	MSA
Mercer	Somerset	22 Jun 1804			F
			Marriage Intentions	1769-1891	MSA
Merrill	Aroostook	5 Mar 1895	1938-	1893-	Ind
Mexico	Oxford	13 Feb 1818	1818-	1883-	Ind/F
				1818-1892	
Milbridge	Washington	14 Jul 1848	1848-	1892-	Ind
			1848-1891	1848-1891	MSA
Milburn (see Skowhegan)					
Milford	Penobscot	28 Feb 1833	1952-	1864-	F
			Marriages	1864-1891	MSA
Millinocket	Penobscot	16 Mar 1901	1901-	1898-	
Milo	Piscataquis	21 Jan 1823	1823-	1823-	Ind
				1802-1891	MSA
Minot	Androscoggin	21 Jan 1823	1802-	1795-	
				1786-1891	MSA
Monhegan Plantation	Lincoln	4 Sep 1839	1840s-	1900-	Inc
			1841-1889	1841-1889	MSA
Monmouth	Kennebec	20 Jan 1792	1888-	1800s-	Ind/F
			1774-1892	1774-1892	MSA
Monroe	Waldo	12 Feb 1818	1820-	1812-	Ind
				1778-1892	MSA
Monson	Piscataquis	8 Feb 1822	1920-	1911-	Ind/F
				1635-1890	MSA
Montgomery (see Troy)					
Monticello	Aroostook	29 Jul 1846		1892-	
			1860-1896	1860-1896	MSA
Montville	Waldo	18 Feb 1807	1802-	1807-	Ind
			1785-1891	1785-1891	MSA
Moose River	Somerset	16 Oct 1852	1900-	late 1800s-	
Moro Plantation	Aroostook	1850	1922-	1896-	
Morrill	Waldo	3 Mar 1855	1855-	1855-	Ind
				1781-1891	MSA
Moscow	Somerset	30 Jan 1816	1816-	1850-	
				1771-1892	MSA
Mount Chase Plantation	Penobscot	21 Mar 1864	1951-	1871-	Ind
Mount Desert	Hancock	17 Feb 1789	1900-	1894-	
				1806-1932	MSA

TOWN	COUNTY	ORGANIZED	TOWN RECORDS	VITAL RECORDS	CODES
Mount Vernon	Kennebec	28 Jun 1792	1797-	1892-	F
				1775-1903	MSA
Naples	Cumberland	4 Mar 1834	1834-	1892-	
				1834-1891	MSA
Nashville Plantation	Aroostook	17 Apr 1889	1889-	1889-	
New Canada	Aroostook	9 Nov 1881	1892-	1892-	
New Charleston (see Charleston)					
New Gloucester	Cumberland	9 Mar 1774	1700-	1700-	Ind
				1771-1892	MSA
New Limerick	Aroostook	18 Mar 1837	1861-	1892-	
New Milford (see Alna)					
New Portland	Somerset	9 Mar 1808	1836-	1892-	F
				1770-1892	MSA
New Sharon	Franklin	20 Jun 1794	1800s-	1891-	Ind/F
				1797-1953	
New Sweden	Aroostook	29 Jan 1895		1895-	F
				1872-1900	
New Vineyard	Franklin	22 Feb 1802		1892-	F
Newburgh	Penobscot	15 Feb 1819	1814-	1814-	F
				1828-1939	MSA
Newcastle	Lincoln	19 Jun 1753	1892-	1892-	Ind
			1754-1891	1754-1891	MSA
Newfield	York	26 Feb 1794	1900	1897-	Ind/F
Newport	Penobscot	14 Jun 1814	1835-1850;1866-	1892-	Ind/Inc
				1858-1891	MSA
Newry	Oxford	15 Jun 1805	1805-	1810-	
			1805-1894	1805-1894	MSA
Nobleboro	Lincoln	20 Nov 1788	1788-	1914-	Ind/F
			1788-1891	1788-1891	MSA
Norridgewock	Somerset	18 Jun 1788	1950s-	1620-	Ind
			1674-1892	1674-1892	MSA
North Berwick	York	22 Mar 1831	1831-	1892-	
			1831-1892	1831-1892	MSA
North Haven	Knox	30 Jun 1846	1846-	1892-	
			1802-1891	1802-1891	MSA
North Hill (see Brighton Plantation)					
North Yarmouth	Cumberland	1732 ?	1732-	1720-	Ind/Inc
Northfield	Washington	21 Mar 1838	1938-	1838-	F
				1798-1907	MSA
Northport	Waldo	13 Feb 1796		1896-	Ind/F
Norway	Oxford	9 Mar 1797	1856-	1890-	F
				1700-1892	MSA
Number 14 Plantation	Washington	5 Mar 1895		1875-	Ind
Number 21 Plantation	Washington	5 Mar 1895	1899-	1892-	
Oakfield	Aroostook	24 Feb 1897	1897-	1892-	Ind
				1882-1891	MSA
Oakland	Kennebec	26 Feb 1873	1873-	1873-	
Ogunquit	York	1 Jul 1980			
(Formerly part of the Town of Wells)					
				1871-1892	MSA

TOWN	COUNTY	ORGANIZED	TOWN RECORDS	VITAL RECORDS	CODES
Old Orchard Beach	York	20 Feb 1883	1883-	1883-	Ind/Inc
Old Town	Penobscot	16 Mar 1840	1840-	1820-	Ind
				1820-1891	MSA
Orient	Aroostook	9 Apr 1856		1892-	F
Orland	Hancock	21 Feb 1800	1792-	1770-	Inc
				1765-1920	MSA
Orono	Penobscot	12 Mar 1806	1806-	1806-	Ind/F
			1806-1907	1806-1907	MSA
Orrington	Penobscot	21 Mar 1788	1788-	1700s-Ind	
			1643-1887	1643-1893	MSA
Osborn	Hancock	5 Mar 1895		1938-	
Otis	Hancock	19 Mar 1835	1962-	1898-	Inc
			1835-1955	1835-1955	MSA
Otisfield	Cumberland	19 Feb 1798	1798-	1798-	
Owl's Head	Knox	9 Jul 1921	1921-	1921-	
Oxbow Plantation	Aroostook	5 Mar 1895	1940-	1940-	F
Oxford	Oxford	27 Feb 1829	1892-	1892-	Ind/F
				1829-1857	MSA
Palermo	Waldo	23 Jun 1804	1831-	1908-	Ind/F
Palmyra	Somerset	20 Jun 1807	1807-	1892-	
				1800-1892	MSA
Paris	Oxford	20 Jun 1793	1829	1700-	Ind
			1793-1906	1795-1902	MSA
Parkman	Piscataquis	29 Jan 1822	1822-	1822-	
				1782-1891	MSA
Parsonfield	York	9 Mar 1785	1785- late	1700s-	
			1774-1969	1762-1948	MSA
Passadumdeag	Penobscot	31 Jan 1835	1935-	1890-	Ind
				1844-1954	MSA
Patten	Penobscot	16 Apr 1841	1841-	1860s-	Ind/F
				1821-1918	MSA
Pembroke	Washington	4 Feb 1832	1832-	1892-	Ind/F
				1831-1892	MSA
Penobscot	Hancock	23 Feb 1787	1880-	1892-	
				1732-1892	MSA
Pepperrellborough (see Saco)					
Perham	Aroostook	21 Feb 1878	1897-	1897-	
				1855-1891	MSA
Perry	Washington	12 Feb 1818	1965-	1818-	Ind
				1780-1891	MSA
Peru	Oxford	5 Feb 1821	1821-	1812-	
				1813-1897	MSA
Phillips	Franklin	25 Feb 1812	1812-	1762-	Ind/Inc
				1763-1891	MSA
Phillipsburg (see Hollis)					
Phippsburg	Sagadahoc	26 Jan 1814	1814-	1807-	
				1825-1891	MSA
Pittsfield	Somerset	19 Jun 1819	1819-1880;1900-	1816-	Ind
			1815-1891	1815-1891	MSA
Pittsdon	Kennebec	4 Feb 1779	1777-	1777-	Ind/F
			1785-1841	1785-1914	MSA

TOWN	COUNTY	ORGANIZED	TOWN RECORDS	VITAL RECORDS	CODES
Pleasant Point	Washington	(information not available)			
Pleasant Ridge					
Plantation	Somerset	5 Mar 1895	1852-	1892-	F
			1852-1897	1852-1897	MSA
Plymouth	Penobscot	21 Feb 1826	1932-	1823-	F
				1795-1891	MSA
Poland	Androscoggin	17 Feb 1795		1700-	Ind
		Proprietor's Records 1734-1798		1780-1937	MSA
Port Watson (see Brooklin)					
Portage Lake	Aroostook	5 Mar 1895	1909-	1892-	
			1875-1892	1875-1892	MSA
Porter	Oxford	20 Feb 1807	1829-	1892-	
Portland	Cumberland	4 Jul 1786	1786-	1714-	Ind
			1786-1882	1712-1904	MSA
Pownal	Cumberland	3 Mar 1808	1808-	1808-	Ind/Inc
			1800-1892	1800-1892	MSA
Pownalborough (see Wiscasset)					
Prentiss					
Plantation	Penobscot	27 Feb 1858	1900s-	1880s-	F
				1841-1939	MSA
Presque Isle	Aroostook	4 Apr 1859	1892-	1892-	Ind/F
				1859-1892	MSA
Princeton	Washington	3 Feb 1832	1960-	1892-	F
				1861-1889	MSA
Prospect	Waldo	24 Feb 1794	1889-	1832-	Ind/F
				1756-1891	MSA
Putnam (see Washington)					
Randolph	Kennebec	4 Mar 1887	1922-	1898-	Ind
Rangeley	Franklin	29 Mar 1855	1855-	1892-	Ind
				1795-1892	MSA
Rangeley					
Plantation	Franklin	5 Mar 1895	1900-	1910-	
Raymond	Cumberland	21 Jun 1803	1803-	1800-	Ind/F
				1745-1916	MSA
Readfield	Kennebec	11 Mar 1791	1790s-	1791-	
				1777-1892	MSA
Reed					
Plantation	Aroostook	21 Feb 1878	1800-	1892-	
Richmond	Sagadahoc	10 Feb 1823	1823-	1892-	Ind
				1782-1892	MSA
Ripley	Somerset	11 Dec 1816	1892-	1892-	Ind/F
				1783-1892	MSA
Rockabema (See Moro Plantation)					
Robbinston	Washington	18 Feb 1811	1886-	1886-	Ind
				1857-1937	MSA
Rockland	Knox	28 Jul 1848	1854-	1892-	Ind
				1803-1892	MSA
Rockport	Knox	17 Feb 1891	1791-	1791-	Ind/Inc
			1783-1892	1783-1892	MSA
Rome	Kennebec	7 Mar 1804			F
			1776-1892	1776-1892	MSA
Roque Bluffs	Washington	12 Mar 1891	1891-	1892-	
Roxbury	Oxford	17 Mar 1835		1892-	

TOWN	COUNTY	ORGANIZED	TOWN RECORDS	VITAL RECORDS	CODES
Rumford	Oxford	21 Feb 1800	1800-	1800-	Ind
				1800-1892	MSA
Sabattus	Androscoggin	7 Mar 1840	1700s-	1892-	
Saco	York	15 Jun 1762	1867-	1762-1867	Ind
				1717-1898	MSA
Saint Agatha	Aroostook	17 Mar 1899	1889-	1889-	Ind
Saint Albans	Somerset	14 Jun 1813	1914-	1813-	Ind/F
				1785-1892	MSA
Saint Francis	Aroostook	12 Mar 1870	1892-	1892-	
Saint George	Knox	7 Feb 1803	1803-	1700-	
				1737-1891	MSA
Saint John Plantation	Aroostook	12 Mar 1870	1950-	1885-	
Sandy River Plantation	Franklin	23 Mar 1905	1905-	1895-	
Sanford	York	27 Feb 1768	1877-	1892-	
			1661-1907	1769-1907	MSA
Sangerville	Piscataquis	13 Jun 1814	1814-	1814-	
				1793-1885	MSA
Scarborough	Cumberland	14 Jul 1658	1681-	1700s-	Ind
			1725-1893	1725-1891	MSA
Searsmont	Waldo	5 Feb 1814	1814-	1854-	Ind/F
				1854-1891	MSA
Searsport	Waldo	13 Feb 1845	1845-	1892-	Ind
				1801-1939	MSA
Sebago	Cumberland	10 Feb 1826		1892-	F
Sebasticook	(See Benton)				
Sebec	Piscataquis	28 Feb 1812	1794-	1811-	Ind/Inc
				1813-1853	MSA
Seboeis Plantation	Penobscot	5 Mar 1895	1890-	c1890-	
Sedgwick	Hancock	14 Jan 1789	1789-	1789-	Ind/F
				1792-1927	MSA
Shapleigh	York	5 Mar 1785	1785- 1785-1873; 1892-		
			1784-1896	1784-1896	MSA
Sherman	Aroostook	28 Jan 1862	1904-	1862-	Ind/F
				1800-1892	MSA
Shirley	Piscataquis	4 Mar 1834	1896-	1890-	Ind/F
				1797-1883	MSA
Sidney	Kennebec	30 Jan 1792	1700-	1800s-	F
				1772-1892	MSA
Skowhegan	Somerset	5 Feb 1823	1814-	1780-	Ind/F
			Index to births	1803-1953	MSA
Smithfield	Somerset	28 Feb 1840	1850-	1775-	Ind/F
			1775-1898	1775-1898	MSA
Smyrna	Aroostook	7 Mar 1839	1866-	1895-	Ind
			1869-1909	1869-1909	MSA
Solon	Somerset	23 Feb 1809	1804-	1700-	
				1764-1916	MSA
Somerville	Lincoln	25 Mar 1858	1853-	1883-	
				1798-1892	MSA
Sorrento	Hancock	8 Mar 1895	1940s-	1859-	Ind

MAINE

TOWN	COUNTY	ORGANIZED	TOWN RECORDS	VITAL RECORDS	CODES
South Berwick	York	12 Feb 1814	1814-	1814-	F
			1763-1892	1763-1892	MSA
South Bristol	Lincoln	26 Mar 1915	1916-	1916-	
South Portland	Cumberland	15 Mar 1895	1933-	1761-	Ind
			1748-1865	1748-1865	MSA
South Thomaston	Knox	28 Jul 1848	1848-	1893-	Ind
			1780-1893	1780-1893	MSA
Southport	Lincoln	12 Feb 1842	1842-	1892-	F
			1842-1892	1842-1892	MSA
Southwest Harbor	Hancock	21 Feb 1905	1905-	1905-	Ind
Springfield	Penobscot	12 Feb 1834	1834-1878;1903-	1898-	Inc
				1834-1897	MSA
Stacyville	Penobscot	7 Mar 1883	1874-	1872-	F
			1860-1876	1860-1876	MSA
Standish	Cumberland	30 Nov 1785	1785-	1790-	Ind/Inc
			1785-1892	1770-1939	MSA
Starks	Somerset	28 Feb 1795	1796-	1796-	
				1787-1892	MSA
Stetson	Penobscot	28 Jan 1831	1900-	1800s-	Ind/F
				1803-1894	MSA
Steuben	Washington	27 Feb 1795	1795-	1795-1868;1893-	Ind/Inc
				1769-1900	MSA
Stockholm	Aroostook	27 Feb 1911	1891-	1897-	Ind
Stockton Springs	Waldo	13 Mar 1857	1857-	1857-	
				1832-1891	MSA
Stoneham	Oxford	31 Jan 1834	1912-	1892-	F
				1837-1890	MSA
Stonington	Hancock	18 Feb 1897	1897-	1897-	Ind
Stow	Oxford	28 Jan 1833	1830-	1830-	Ind
Strong	Franklin	31 Jan 1801	1801-	1767-	
			1779-1892	1779-1892	MSA
Stroudwater	(See Westbrook)				
Sullivan	Hancock	16 Feb 1789	1795-	1892-	Ind
			1745-1891	1745-1891	MSA
Sumner	Oxford	13 Jun 1798		1833-	
				1733-1892	MSA
Surry	Hancock	21 Jun 1803	1800s-	1700s-	Ind
				1790-1938	MSA
Swan's Island	Hancock	26 Mar 1897	1839-	1850-	Ind/Inc
Swanville	Waldo	19 Feb 1818	1814-	1800s-	
				1812-1891	MSA
Sweden	Oxford	26 Feb 1813	1953-	1953-	F
Talmadge	Washington	8 Feb 1875	1850-	1850-	
				1850-1893	MSA/Inc
Temple	Franklin	20 Jun 1803	1803-	1803-	Ind
				1784-1892	MSA
Thomaston	Knox	20 Mar 1777	1776-	1776-	Ind
				1775-1893	MSA
Thompsonborough	(See Lisbon)				

MAINE

TOWN	COUNTY	ORGANIZED	TOWN RECORDS	VITAL RECORDS	CODES
Thorndike	Waldo	15 Feb 1819	1819-	1892-	Ind/Inc
				1776-1894	MSA
Topsfield	Washington	24 Feb 1838	1860-	1860-	Inc
				1834-1892	MSA
Topsham	Sagadahoc	4 Feb 1764	1926-	1892-	Inc
Townsend	(See Southport)				
Tremont	Hancock	3 Jun 1848	1848-	1853-	Ind
				1825-1892	MSA
Trenton	Hancock	16 Feb 1789	1901-	1900-	
			1786-1891	1786-1891	MSA
Troy	Waldo	22 Feb 1812	1812-	1812-	
				1840-1891	MSA
Turner	Androscoggin	7 Jul 1786	1785-	1776-	Ind
			1787-1892	1776-1896	MSA
			Index to Vital Records	1740-1955	MSA
Union	Knox	20 Oct 1786	1788-	1795-	Ind/F
				1789-1914	MSA
Unity	Waldo	22 Jun 1804	1804-	1790-	
				1797-1864	MSA
Upton	Oxford	9 Feb 1860	1830s-	1892-	
Usher	(See Stoneham)				
Van Buren	Aroostook	11 Feb 1881	1881-	1838-	Ind/F
				1838-1893	MSA
Vanceboro	Washington	4 Mar 1874	1938-	1814-	Inc
Vassalboro	Kennebec	26 Apr 1771	1700-	1815-	Ind
			1764-1892	1764-1892	MSA
Veazie	Penobscot	26 Mar 1853	1853-	1850-	Ind
				1852-1894	MSA
Verona	Hancock	18 Feb 1861	1955-	1900-	F
Vienna	Kennebec	20 Feb 1802	1802-	1802-	
				1752-1893	MSA
Vinalhaven	Knox	25 Jun 1789	1789-	1790-	Ind
			1785-1892	1785-1892	MSA
Wade	Aroostook	4 Mar 1913	1949-	1899-	Ind/Inc
Waite	Washington	22 Feb 1876		1892-	Ind/Inc
Waldo	Waldo	17 Mar 1845		1892-	Ind/F
Waldoboro	Lincoln	29 Jun 1773	1773-	1892-	
			1778-1892	1778-1892	MSA
Wales	Androscoggin	1 Feb 1816	1836-1858;1921-	1730s-	Ind/F
				1759-1900	MSA
Wallagrass Plantation	Aroostook	12 Mar 1870	1838-	1892-	F
			1866-1894	1866-1894	MSA
Waltham	Hancock	29 Jan 1833	1890-	1850-	
Warren	Knox	7 Nov 1776	1776-	1845-	Ind
				1795-1938	MSA
Warsaw	(See Pittsfield)				
Washburn	Aroostook	25 Feb 1861	1912-	1898-	Ind/F
				1885-1891	MSA
Washington	Knox	27 Feb 1811	1811-	1812-	Ind/F
				1800-1891	
Waterboro	York	6 Mar 1787	1787-	1860-	Ind/F
			1787-1876	1787-1891	MSA

TOWN	COUNTY	ORGANIZED	TOWN RECORDS	VITAL RECORDS	CODES
Waterford	Oxford	2 Mar 1797	1798-	1762-	Inc
				1762-1859	MSA
Waterville	Kennebec	23 Jun 1802	1802-	1830s-	Ind
				1813-1893	MSA
			Index to Vital Records	1830-1943	MSA
Wayne	Kennebec	12 Feb 1798	1819-	1770-	F
			1773-1900	1773-1900	MSA
Webster (See Sabbatus)					
Webster Plantation	Penobscot	1 Sep 1856	1920-	1892-	
				1840-1891	MSA
Weld	Franklin	8 Feb 1816	1844-	1761-	Ind
				1766-1895	MSA
Wellington	Piscataquis	23 Feb 1828	1828-	1898-	Ind/F
			1823-1892	1823-1892	MSA
Wells	York	30 Aug 1653	1700s-	1600s-	Ind/F
				1695-1900	MSA
Wesley	Washington	24 Jan 1833	1832-	1776-	
			Births and deaths	1887-1891	MSA
			Marriages	1840-1846	MSA
West Bath	Sagadahoc	14 Feb 1844	1914-	1845-	Inc
				1845-1936	MSA
West Forks Plantation	Somerset	31 Mar 1893	1898-	1898-	F
West Gardiner	Kennebec	8 Aug 1850		1850-	Ind
				1848-1892	MSA
West Paris	Oxford	28 Aug 1957	1958-	1958-	Ind
West Pittston (See Randolph)					
West Waterville (See Oakland)					
Westbrook	Cumberland	14 Feb 1814	1718-	1892-	Ind
				1800-1892	MSA
Westfield	Aroostook	7 Mar 1905	1894-1904;1912-	1892-	Ind/Inc
Westmanland Plantation	Aroostook	5 Mar 1895	1940s-	1892-	
Weston	Aroostook	17 Mar 1835	1835-	1835-	Ind
				1814-1892	MSA
Westport	Lincoln	5 Feb 1828		1892-	F
			1761-1945	1761-1945	MSA
Whitefield	Lincoln	19 Jun 1809	1791-	1700s-	Ind/F
			1748-1892	1748-1892	MSA
Whiting	Washington	15 Feb 1825	1817-	1820s-	
				1814-1891	MSA
Whitneyville	Washington	10 Feb 1845	1890-	1890-	Ind/F
				1861-1891	MSA
Willimantic	Piscataquis	22 Feb 1881	1881-	1800s-	
				1859-1939	MSA
Wilton	Franklin	22 Jun 1803	1949-	1783-	Ind/Inc
			1765-1891	1765-1891	MSA
Windham	Cumberland	12 Jun 1762	1762-	1837-	Ind/Inc
			1823-1892	1789-1921	MSA
Windsor	Kennebec	3 Mar 1809	1894-	1870-	Ind/F
			1797-1834	1797-1892	MSA

TOWN	COUNTY	ORGANIZED	TOWN RECORDS	VITAL RECORDS	CODES
Winn	Penobscot	21 Mar 1857	1892-	1872-	Inc
				1872-1917	MSA
Winslow	Kennebec	26 Apr 1771	1771-	1759-	Ind/Inc
			1771-1891	1771-1891	MSA
Winter Harbor	Hancock	21 Feb 1895	1895-	1895-	Ind
Winterport	Waldo	12 Mar 1860	1860-	1860-	Ind/Inc
				1860-1894	MSA
Winterville Plantation	Aroostook	5 Mar 1895	1884-	1883-	
				1876-1949	MSA
Winthrop	Kennebec	26 Apr 1771	1800s-	1890-	Ind
				1720-1908	MSA
Wiscasset	Lincoln	13 Feb 1760	1760-	1790-	Ind
			1752-1945	1752-1945	MSA
Woodland	Aroostook	5 Mar 1880	1875-	1875-	Ind/F
				1874-1891	MSA
Woodstock	Oxford	7 Feb 1815	1815-	1815-	
			1815-1908	1814-1908	MSA
Woodville	Penobscot	28 Feb 1895	1930-	1900-	F
Woolwich	Sagadahoc	20 Oct 1759	1871-	1752-	Ind
			1760-1828	1756-1895	MSA
Yarmouth	Cumberland	20 Aug 1849	1800s-	1815-	Ind
			1849-1892	1830-1910	MSA
York	York	22 Nov 1652	1897-	1832-	Ind
				1715-1877	MSA

****

CENSUS RECORDS - FEDERAL

The federal census through 1850 is available on microfilm at the Maine State Library, but all extant returns are available in the Archives as well. All returns are on microfilm at the Archives and originals for 1850 through 1880 are at the Archives. The 1880 returns are made available only when a reading from the microfilm is doubtful. The entire county of Waldo is available in an indexed typescript at the Archives and also at the Belfast Public Library.

Federal census schedules for the entire United States are at the National Archives - Boston Branch in Waltham, Massachusetts. (See entry under Massachusetts - Census Records - Federal.)

CENSUS RECORDS - STATE

The only Maine State Census was taken in 1837. Besides Bangor and Portland, several unorganized townships in Washington (including parts of present-day Aroostook) also survive in the Archives, and the Eliot section is at Portland at the Maine Historical Society.

****

PROBATE AND LAND RECORDS

PROBATE RECORDS (Wills, Administrations, etc.) and LAND RECORDS for Maine are
held at the County seat. Offices usually are open from 8:30-5:00 on Mondays
through Fridays, but check times! Some do not open until 9:00

ANDROSCOGGIN COUNTY   (established in 1854 from Cumberland, Oxford and Kennebec
    Court House   Counties)
    2 Turner Street
    Auburn, ME 04210
    Register of Probate   782-0281   Probate Records, 1854-present.
                                                  Indexed
    Register of Deeds   782-0191   Land Records, 1854-present.

AROOSTOOK COUNTY   (established in 1839 from Washington County)
    <u>Southern Registry</u>   (includes Probate Records for entire county)
    Court Street   P.O. Box 787
    Houlton, ME 04730
    Register of Probate   532-7317 Ext 122 Probate Records, 1840-present.
                                                    Indexed
    Register of Deeds   532-7317 Ext 101 Deeds*, 1808-present. Indexed
     *Register has copies of all Washington Co. deeds to Aroostook Co. land
      recorded before the creation of the county.

    <u>Northern Registry</u>
    Fort Kent, ME 04743   834-3925   Deeds, 1846-present. Indexed.

CUMBERLAND COUNTY   (established 1760 from York County)
    Court House
    142 Federal Street
    Portland, ME 04101-4196   773-2931   Probate Records, 1908-present.
    Register of Probate   Indexed on cards. Microfilmed
                                             Search by mail: $10/record
    Register of Deeds   773-6493   Deeds, 1760-present. Indexed.
                                             Microfilmed. Staff-operated
                                           photocopying. $1 1st page.
                                           Service by mail.

FRANKLIN COUNTY   (established 1838 from Cumberland County)
    Court House
    Main Street
    Farmington, ME 04938
    Register of Probate   778-2620   Probate Records, 1838-present.
                                                  Indexed.
    Register of Deeds   778-2818   Deeds, 1838-present. Indexed.

HANCOCK COUNTY   (established 1789 from Lincoln County)
    Court House
    60 State Street
    Ellsworth, ME 04605
    Register of Probate   667-8434   Probate Records, 1790-present.
                                                  Indexed.
    Register of Deeds   667-8353   Deeds, 1790-present. Indexed.

KENNEBEC COUNTY   (established 1799 from Lincoln County)
    Court House
    95 State Street
    Augusta, ME 04330   Probate Records, 1799-present.
    Register of Probate   622-7559   Indexed. Microfilmed.
                                               Deeds, 1799-present. Indexed.
    Register of Deeds   622-0431   Microfilmed.

KNOX COUNTY   (established 1860 from Lincoln and Waldo Counties)
    Court House
    62 Union Street
    Rockland, ME 04841   Probate Records, 1860-present.
    Register of Probate   594-4915   Indexed.
                                               Deeds, 1760-present. Indexed.
    Register of Deeds   594-4061   Microfilmed.

LINCOLN COUNTY   (established 1760 from York County)
    Court House   Probate Records, Nov 1769 to
    High Street   present. Indexed.
    Wiscasset, ME 04578   Deeds, Nov 1768-present.
    Register of Probate   882-7392   Indexed.* Staff-operated
                                               Photocopying $.50/pg.
    Register of Deeds   882-7431   Reader/printer. Serv. by mail.

*The first 80 vols. well indexed. From Vol. 81 to ca1850, index in each vol.
must be searched. Index alphabetical by 1st letter of surname only. County
records also include Naturalization Records, Rev. War Pensioners, etc.

OXFORD COUNTY   (established 1805 from York and Cumberland Counties)
    Court House
    26 Western Ave. P.O. Box 179   Probate Records, 1820-present
    South Paris, ME 04281   (some records prior to 1820).
    Register of Probate   743-6671   Indexed.
                                               Deeds, Eastern Registery,
    Register of Deeds   743-6211   So. Paris. 1805-present. Ind.
                                               Deeds, Western Registery
                                               Fryeburg 04037. 1800-present.
                                               Indexed.

PENOBSCOT COUNTY   (established 1816 from Hancock County)
    Court House
    97 Hammond Street
    Bangor, ME 04401
    Register of Probate   942-8542   Probate Records, 1816-present.
                                               Indexed.*
    Register of Deeds   942-8539   Deeds, 1814-present. Indexed.

*Separate indexes to wills, admins. & guardianships. Alphabetical by 1st
letter of surname only. Names slowly being computerized for easier use.

PISCATAQUIS COUNTY   (established 1838 from Penobscot and Somerset Counties)
    Court House
    51 East Main Street
    Dover-Foxcroft, ME 04426
    Register of Probate   564-2431   Probate Records, 1838-present.
                                                   Indexed.
    Register of Deeds   564-7708   Deeds, 1838-present. Indexed.

SAGADAHOC COUNTY (established 1854 from Lincoln County)
    Court House
    752 High Street
    Bath, ME 04530   Probate Records, 1954-present.
    Register of Probate   443-2551   Indexed.
                                                   Deeds, 1826-present. Indexed.
    Register of Deeds   443-2441   Staff-operated photocopying.
                                                   Service by mail.

SOMERSET COUNTY   (established 1809 from Kennebec County)
    Court House
    Corner High and Court Streets
    Skowhegan, ME 04976
    Register of Probate   474-3322   Probate Records, 1830-present.
                                                   Indexed.
    Register of Deeds   474-3421   Deeds, 1809-present. Indexed.

WALDO COUNTY   (established 1827 from Hancock County)
    Court House
    73 Church Street
    Belfast, ME 04915
    Register of Probate   338-2780   Probate Records, 1827-present.
                                                   Indexed.
    Register of Deeds   338-1710   Deeds,* 1700s-present. Indexed
    *Register has copies of all Hancock Co. deeds to Waldo Co. land 1789-1827.

WASHINGTON COUNTY   (established 1789 from Lincoln County)
    Court House
    Court Street
    Machias, ME 04654
    Register of Probate   255-6591   Probate, 1785-present. Indexed
    Reigster of Deeds   255-6512   Deeds, 1784-present. Indexed.

YORK COUNTY   (original county)
    Court House
    Court Street. P.O. Box 399   Probate, 1687-present.
    Alfred, ME 04002   324-1577   See Maine Wills to 1760
    Register of Probate   (printed).
                                                   Deeds, 1642-present. Indexed..
    Register of Deeds   324-1576   Microfilmed. (See York Deeds,
                                                   19 vols. to 1737.)

CEMETERY RECORDS

While Maine contains many churchyards, the most frequent place of burial in early years was private property near the residence. Transcripts before WWII of burial grounds were largely the work of organizations such as the DAR. Principal holders of these transcripts are the Maine Historical Society in Portland, the Maine State Library in Augusta, and the New England Historic Genealogical Society in Boston, Massachusetts. Some public libraries have local transcripts not available elsewhere. A comprehensive list of transcripts is being compiled for the Maine Old Cemetery Association.

The Maine State Library in Augusta is a repository for the records of the Surname Index Project (SIP) of the Maine Old Cemetery Association (MOCA). The microfilm index includes names of hundreds of thousands of persons living in Maine between 1650 and 1970. Copies of the index are at NEHGS, Lynnfield Public Library, and other libraries. The reference staff of the State Library will search for individual names in the records, in response to mail requests, and will assist in-house users in their research. There is a .10 per page charge for photocopies. Minimum $1 for out-of-state mail requests.

****

CHURCH RECORDS

Church records of baptisms, marriages and burials are a major untapped source for Maine. Some that precede 1829 exist in most towns - usually marriage records. Published and unpublished manuscripts of Congregational Church registers and of Quaker records are in the Maine Historical Society. Few registers of Episcopal churches and almost no Methodist registers have been transcribed.

****

MILITARY RECORDS

MAINE STATE ARCHIVES   (See entry under MAINE-VITAL RECORDS)

The FOGLER LIBRARY, UNIVERSITY OF MAINE, Orono, is custodian of the Bicentennial Project (BIP) of the Maine Old Cemetery Association (MOCA). This project produced a print-out (Index) in 1977 of veterans of the Revolutionary War who lived in Maine. A photocopy of the note cards will be sent by mail for a $2 fee, plus a long stamped envelope. Copies of the print-out may be consulted in person at the Maine State Library in Augusta, the Maine Historical Society in Portland and the Cutler Library in Farmington.

See the list of printed military records in Frost's Maine Genealogy: A Bibliographical Guide, mentioned under MAINE - BOOKS AND ARTICLES. Since Maine was part of Massachusetts until 1820, books on Massachusetts Military records must be consulted.

****

MAINE

IMMIGRATION AND NATURALIZATION RECORDS

Immigration and Naturalization records are maintained by the court in which the person was naturalized and may be obtained directly from the clerk of the court. There is a card-index to naturalization records for all courts (Federal, State and City) covering the years 1798 to 1906 at the Court House in Portland. After 1906 naturalization became a Federal function and records from that date may be obtained either at the local court house or from the Immigration and Naturalization Service (Dept. of Justice), Washington, D.C. To request a copy of the record from Washington, use the current form which may be obtained from the New England Branch of the National Archives at 380 Trapelo Road, Waltham, Massachusetts. The name, date and court of naturalization must be known. There is a fee for this service.

****

LIBRARIES

There are public libraries in most towns in Maine. Their holdings vary greatly. The majority of them have small collections which may include items of genealogical interest. Many are open 12 hours a week or less and do not have staff to do any research. For a list of all libraries, consult the American Library Directory in most large libraries to see what is available and what hours of service are offered.

AUGUSTA - MAINE STATE ARCHIVES (See entry under MAINE - VITAL RECORDS)

AUGUSTA - MAINE STATE LIBRARY
State House Station 64
Augusta, Maine 04333
207-289-3561
Mon, Wed, Fri 9-5; Tues, Thu 9-9;
Sat. 11-5 (School yr, Sept-June).

From Maine Turnpike Exit 15. (Rte. 202) towards Augusta. At rotary bear right onto Rte. 27 (State St.). First driveway past Capitol.

Self-service photocopying $.10/page. 6 microfilm readers (4 are reader/printers). $.10 per page. Limited research by mail. Genealogy materials do not circulate. Holdings: Reference materials are strongest for Maine, New Hampshire and Massachusetts with some materials on the other N.E. states and French Canada. Published vital records, church records for many New England towns. Maine Census 1800-1850 on microfilm. Indexes for New England State Censuses from 1790-1850. 73 vols. of cemetery transcripts are in the Maine Old Cemetery Association, Maine Index Project. The MOCA Surname Index Project is now available on microfilm only (some 155,000 sheets in alphabetical order). The BIP (Bicentennial Index Project) locating graves of Revolutionary Veterans will soon be issued in its final print-out. There are Miscellaneous DAR Records (typescripts of Bible records, town vital statistics, etc.), the standard textbooks on methodology, the Munsell supplement for works available at the State Library helps to locate buried references (it's the equivalent to Greenlaw at NEHGS), The American Genealogist, The Putnam publications, Mayflower Descendant, National Genealogical Society Quarterly, New England Historical and Genealogical Register, New York Genealogical and Biographical Record, Old Northwest Quarterly, lineage books for DAR and numerous other lineage organizations, composite genealogies, family genealogies, reference works on surnames and heraldry, numerous Burke's publications, American Genealogical Index, American Genealogical and Biographical Index, New England regional histories, state and county histories, and collections of the Maine Historical Society.

BANGOR - BANGOR PUBLIC LIBRARY
145 Harlow Street
Bangor, ME 04401
207-947-8336
Mon-Fri 9-9, Sat 9-5
Summer 9-7 Mon-Fri

From I-95 take Bangor-Brewer exit, (Rte 1) onto Main St. Go through business district. At intersection bear right. At lights turn left onto Harlow St. Past City Hall to Library.

Holdings: Unique collection of family histories; card index to the Bangor Historical Magazine. Part of Charles E. Banks Collection. (Remainder of Banks collection is at NEHGS & Library of Congress)

BATH - MAINE MARITIME MUSEUM (ARCHIVES)
Sewall House
963 Washington Street
Bath, ME 04530
207-443-6311
For research, call for appointment
Mon-Fri.

From I-95 take exit 22 to Rte 1 to Bath. Just before underpass, bear right. Go left over RR tracks to Washington St. Sewall Huse is on right past "Chocolate Church."

Fee: $3 for non-members. Staff-operated photocopying. Holdings: Ships logs, newspapers, family pictures and histories.

BELFAST - BELFAST FREE LIBRARY
46 High Street
Belfast, ME 04915
207-338-3884
Mon, Wed, Thur 9:30-8; Tues, Fri
9:30-5; Sat 9:30-12

Turn right from Rte 1 on to Business District. This becomes High Street.

Holdings: Maine history; Waldo County history books, newspapers, photos; genealogy.

BRUNSWICK - HAWTHORNE-LONGFELLOW LIBRARY
Bowdoin College
Brunswick, ME 04011
207-725-8731
Mon-Sat 8:30 a.m.-12 p.m.
Sunday 10:30 a.m.-12 p.m.
Summer Mon-Fri 8:30-5

From I-95 take exit 22 to Brunswick. Go straight to business district. Turn right on Main St. Go past college. Library is last building on campus on left.

No fees. Mainly for student use. Photocopying service $.05/page. Holdings: Many genealogical books for Maine and New England.

FARMINGDALE - <u>AUGUSTA MAINE STAKE BRANCH GENEALOGICAL LIBRARY</u>
Church of Jesus Christ of Latter-day Saints
4 Hasson Street   From Maine Turnpike, exit at
Farmingdale, ME   Gardiner onto Rte 201. Through
Mailing address: 2 Sylvan Rd,   Gardiner past Agway Store. Left
Hallowell, ME 04347   onto Hasson Street.
207-582-9833 or 207-623-1755
Wed & Thur 6-10 p.m. 1st & 3rd Fri 2-10 p.m. 2nd & 4th Fri 6-10 p.m.

Open to public. No mail or telephone service. 5 microfilm readers. 5 microfiche readers & 1 reader/printer. Use of 1 copying machine. IGI Index on
fiche. Card catalog of holdings in Salt Lake City. Accelerated Index system on
fiche which is helpful in locating lost ancestors in U.S. Family Registry on
microfiche and many research tools also on microfiche.

MACHIASPORT - <u>MACHIASPORT HISTORICAL SOCIETY GATES HOUSE</u>
Machiasport, ME 04655   Take Rte 92 at bottom of College
207-255-8461   Hill. Keep to right. In about
Mon-Fri (June) 12-4 p.m.   miles you come to Machiasport
(July-Sept. 13) 10 a.m.- 4 p.m.   Town Hall on right. On left is
Also open by appointment   Gates House.

No fees. Donations welcome. Early genealogical records of local families.
Census records for Machiasport. Maritime Room with artifacts. Several ships
logs. Marine books in library.

MADAWASKA - <u>MADAWASKA HISTORICAL SOCIETY LIBRARY</u>
Main Street   Mid-town Madawaska on U.S. #1.
Madawaska, ME 04756
207-728-7749
Mon-Fri, 9-8; Sat 1-3

No fee. Microfilm reader. No mail service, no copier. <u>Holdings</u>: French
Canadian & Acadian genealogies, photos, maps; "Acadian Roots." St. John Valley
40-volume Genealogical Collection. Microfilm reader. VRs of New Brunswick.
Maine Census for Aroostook Cty.

ORONO - <u>THE RAYMOND H. FOGLER LIBRARY, SPECIAL COLLECTIONS DEPARTMENT</u>
University of Maine   I-95 to Old Town Stillwater exit.
Orono, ME 04469   Straight through to 3rd lights.
207-581-1686   Right onto College Ave. 1/2 mile
Mon-Sat 8 a.m.- 4:30 p.m.   to campus. Entrance on left.
Sun 1-5 p.m.   Library at end of mall.
Closed Sunday during summer

No Fees. Photocopying service. Microfilm readers. <u>Holdings</u>: Large collection of Maine newspapers on microfilm. Index of Veterans of the Revolutionary War (see entry under Maine - Military Records).

PORTLAND - <u>MAINE HISTORICAL SOCIETY LIBRARY</u>

     485 Congress Street
     Portland, ME 04101
     207-774-1822
     Mon-Fri 9-5

From Maine Turnpike take exit 6-A (I-295). From I-295 take exit 5-A (Congress St.). Continue East on Congress St. through business District. Library on left. Parking garage near library.

Fee: $2 per day for non-members. Photocopying $.25/page. 2 microfilm readers. Materials do not circulate except to members. <u>Holdings</u>: 60,000 printed works on state and family history. 1.7 million manuscript documents. Maine photographs, newspapers, etc. U.S. Census for Maine through 1910 on microfilm.

PORTLAND - <u>PORTLAND PUBLIC LIBRARY</u>

     5 Monument Square
     Portland, ME 04101
     207-773-4761
     Mon, Wed, Fri 9-6
     Tues, Thurs 12-9; Sat 9-5

Monument Square is on Congress St. in the center of the city. Parking garages & lots nearby.

Self-service photocopying $.10/copy. 3 microfilm readers, 2 reader/printers $.20 per copy. Service by mail is limited. <u>Holdings</u>: Maine Collection: materials relating to Maine by subject, author or publisher. Includes town histories, Portland city directories from 1823 and newspapers from 1785. The Library does not specialize in genealogy.

SACO - <u>DYER LIBRARY</u>

     York Institute Museum
     371 Maine Street
     Saco, ME 04072
     207-283-3861 or 207-282-3031
     Mon, Wed, Fri 10-5
     Tues, Thurs 10-8; Sat 9-12

From I-95 take Saco-Old Orchard Beach exit onto Main St. (Rte 1) Go south 3/4 mile. Library and Museum are on the left.

<u>Holdings</u>: 6,000 documents & manuscripts of Saco & York County history. 360 vols. of 18th & 19th century newspapers. Numerous Maine town histories, family genealogies and photos. Ref. sources include <u>York Deeds</u>, <u>Essex Institute Historical Collections</u>, and <u>New England Historical and Genealogical Register</u>. The library has begun an in-house online index to Saco history. The Maine and Saco History room is open Thursdays 1-5 p.m. Photcopying available.

SEARSPORT -<u>STEPHEN PHILLIPS MEMORIAL LIBRARY</u>
     <u>PENOBSCOT MARINE MUSEUM</u>
     Church Street
     Searsport, ME 04974

Church St. is off Rte 1. Library is last building in complex.

Photocopying (Limit 10 copies); Microfilm reader; Mail service; no interlibrary loans. <u>Holdings</u>: Ship registers, photographs, logs, Custom Records, local histories, genealogies, microfilm census and vital records.

SPRINGVALE - SPRINGVALE PUBLIC LIBRARY
226 Main Street   Main St. is Rte 109.
Springvale, ME 04083   On-street parking.
Mon-Fri 11-8; Sat 11-5

Photocopying $.10/copy. Most materials do not circulate. No interlibrary loan
on genealogical materials. Microfilm reader. Mail answered if accompanied by
a SASE. No research fee. Holdings: Strong collection of York County town
histories; family genealogies; Sanford vital records, including cemetery
records; Sanford town reports and city directories; early American immigrants;
military records; census records for York County on microfilm; early Sanford and
Springvale newspapers, historic photos of Sanford & Springvale; bound vols. of
Spragues Journal and Old Eliot.

WELLS - WELLS-OGUNQUIT HISTORICAL SOCIETY LIBRARY
P.O. Box 801, Post Road   From Maine Turnpike, exit 2, take
Wells, ME 04090   left on Rte 109. Follow to end
207-646-4775   & take right onto Rte 1 south.
Summer: Wed. 1-4   Library at First Historic Church
or by appointment   just past 1st set of lights.

Holdings: Strong collection of early Wells genealogies, town, church and
cemetery records. Copy of Wells 1850 Census and Rev. War pension records.
Excellent collection of local and state historical newspaper items & pictures.
Fees: $5 minimum donation for local research & search fee. Copying extra.

****

SOCIETIES

MAINE GENEALOGICAL SOCIETY
P.O. Box 221   Thomas H. Roderick, Ph.D., C.G.,
Farmington, ME 04938   President

Founded in 1976 "to collect, preserve, and publish genealogical records, related
documents and information, to establish and maintain a genealogical library for
the use of those interested in the subject, and to promote and encourage
interest in genealogy of the state of Maine."

Membership: Individual: New member $12 (renewal $7.50). Family: New member
$15 (renewal $10). Benefactor: $40.

1000 active members in 50 states, all the Canadian provinces & several foreign
countries. Four meetings a year rotate around the state in April, June,
September, and November. The annual meeting is always held in Farmington in
September. There are chapters in Waterville, Farmington (Sandy River), Greater
Portland, Augusta, Bangor, and several other local groups may be organized.
A growing collection of library materials is at the Cutler Memorial Library in
Farmington. Publication is the bi-monthly Maine Seine, included with dues. One
query per newsletter is free to members. Inquire: Leon Keyser, 1350 Forest
Ave., Apt. 12, Portland, ME 04103 (207-797-3906). Send ancestor tables (TAG-
style through number 63) to Alan H. Hawkins, 14 Adelbert St., South Portland, ME
04106.

MAINE HISTORICAL SOCIETY
    (See description under MAINE-LIBRARIES)

$20 annual dues. Annual meeting. Place rotates.

Publication: Maine Historical Society Quarterly, available only with
membership. No queries accepted. Articles must relate to Maine history.
Scattered issues available. The Maine Historical Society has also published 6
volumes of Maine, Province and Court Records.

MAINE OLD CEMETERY ASSOCIATION (MOCA)
    P.O. Box 324   Evelin Grover, contact person.
    Augusta, ME 04330

Founded in 1969 "dedicated to the preservation of Maine's neglected cemeteries."
Dues: $3 per year, to Amanda Bond, 8 Greenway Ave., Springvale, ME 04083.
Corresponding Secretary: Hilda M. Fife, 6 Sherwood Drive, Eliot, ME 03903.

Projects: Bicentennial Project (BIP) (See MAINE-MILITARY RECORDS); MOCA Index
Project (MIP) - A compilation of cemetery listings throughout the state. Series
I & II are microfilmed and available in many libraries. The Maine State Library
holds original bound copies.

YORK COUNTY GENEALOGICAL SOCIETY
    P.O. Box 2242
    Ogunquit, ME 03907

Founded in 1985 "to share and mutually assist in the research of family
genealogy, also, to locate, compile and make available genealogical source data
pertaining to York County."

Dues: $10 individual; $15 family. Meetings: Ten regular meetings on the
fourth Wednesday of each month except in July and December. Quarterly
publication planned to begin in the fall of 1985. .All correspondence concerning
queries, membership, etc. should be accompanied by a SASE.

****

PERIODICALS

DOWNEAST ANCESTRY
    P.O. Box 398   Editors: Mary H. Dormer,
    Machias, ME 04654   Rosemary E. Bachelor

Subscription: $15 per year. 6 issues including index. Started June 1977.
Back copies available in Maine State Library, Maine Historical Society Library,
or by contacting editors. Queries free. Must include one Maine location and
one Maine name. May not repeat in a year. Articles and photographs are welcome.

MAINE SEINE (See entry under SOCIETIES - MAINE GENEALOGICAL SOCIETY)

THE SECOND BOAT (Same address & editors as Downeast Ancestry)

Subscription: $12 per year. 4 issues including index. Started May 1980. Specializes in Colonial American Genealogy - especially those that came before 1650 but were not on the "first boat" (The Mayflower). Queries free. Accepts family genealogies, lineage summaries, ancestral charts, old family Bible records, old letters, copies of wills and deeds, and any data pertaining to ancestors who lived in the U.S. prior to 1800.

****
BOOKS AND ARTICLES

Attwood, Stanley Bearce. The Length and Breadth of Maine (Lewiston, Maine, 1946; reprinted Orono: University of Maine Study No. 96, 1973)

Doane, Gilbert H. Searching for Your Ancestors 3rd edition. Appendix A, Section 6.

Fisher, Carleton E. and Sue G. Soldiers, Sailors and Patriots of the Revolutionary War Maine (Louisville, KY: National Society of the Sons of the American Revolution, 1982)

Frost, John E. Maine Genealogy: A Bibliographical Guide. Revised edition (Portland, Maine: The Maine Historical Society, 1985)

Frost, John E. "Maine Genealogy: Some Distinctive Aspects" in The New England Historical and Genealogical Register, 131 (1974) 243-266, and in Genealogical Research in New England, Genealogical Publishing Co., 1984.

Maine: A Bibliography of Its History, ed. by John D. Haskell (Boston: G.K. Hall & Co., 1977) Review by John E. Frost in NEHGR 132 (1978): 146-148.

Varney, George J. A Gazetteer of the State of Maine (Boston: B. B. Russell, 1881 and 1886).

Wright, Norman Edgar. Genealogy in America (Vol. I: Massachusetts, Connecticut and Maine). Salt Lake City, UT: Deseret Book Co., 1968.

****

MASSACHUSETTS

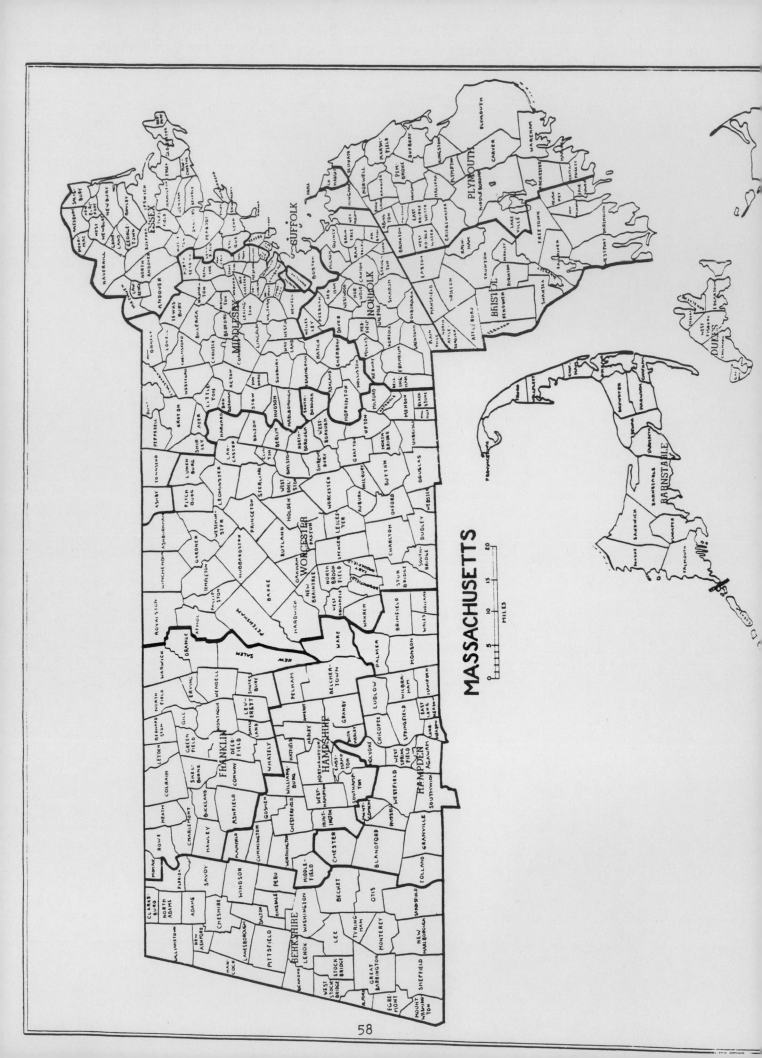

MASSACHUSETTS

MILES
0 5 10 15 20

MASSACHUSETTS

Massachusetts was the first state to be permanently settled and was also the first state to establish laws governing public record keeping. Its colonial records, therefore, are of interest to genealogists throughout the country. However, unlike Connecticut, no one agency has taken the initiative to collect all types of records in one location, and for the beginning genealogist, finding the location of particular records is a study in itself. One of the most complete collections of genealogical printed works and manuscripts is in a private library - the New England Historic Genealogical Society Library in Boston, where there is a $10 per day fee for non-members. Boston Public Library has fine collections of materials of interest to genealogists, but they are scattered throughout several different departments, and the novice can become discouraged. The State Library also has a great deal of material of interest, but no attempt has been made to do the comprehensive job that other New England states have accomplished. Probate and land records must be consulted at the county seats. Again, no one agency has attempted to compile these records on a state-wide basis. Nevertheless, Massachusetts has a great wealth of material available for research. In some instances, its records are the most complete of any state in the Union.

****

VITAL RECORDS TO 1850

In the early-to-mid 1900s, the VITAL RECORDS TO 1850 for 206 of the 364 cities and towns of Massachusetts were published under a state-sponsored program, and copies were deposited in libraries across the state. Today only the major libraries have preserved complete sets of the volumes in the series. However, most libraries have the volumes for their local areas. These bound volumes are uneven in quality, but the majority were carefully done and include not only civil Vital Records but also cemetery, church and Bible records as well. Some volumes of Vital Records were compiled after the "official state series" and not all of these followed the format of the state series. The Society of Mayflower Descendants has published Vital Records for many towns in Plymouth and Barnstable Counties in their Mayflower Descendant and most of these records have been published with indexing by Leonard H. Smith of Clearwater, Florida. In recent years, the Rhode Island Society of Mayflower Descendants has published in book form the Vital Records for Falmouth, Marshfield and Yarmouth, and NEHGS has published volumes for Charlestown and Pepperell. Other Vital Records have been published in the New England Historical and Genealogical Register. Manuscript and typescript copies of Vital Records are available in many libraries across the state. The New England Historic Genealogical Society acquired in 1965 the Walter E. Corbin Manuscript Collection of Town and Vital Records for many towns in Berkshire, Franklin, Hampshire and Hampden Counties. They also have miscellaneous manuscript and typescript records. A few are restricted to use by members. The Berkshire Athenaeum in Pittsfield is custodian of the Rollin H. Cooke Collection which includes church, town and cemetery records for all towns in Berkshire County and other towns in surrounding counties. The Athenaeum has other manuscript material as well. Springfield City Library has manuscript copies of Vital Records for Springfield and Wilbraham,

and cemetery records for other communities. In 1979, the Microfilming Corpora-
tion of America offered for sale on microfiche all of the available published
Massachusetts Vital Records, thus making the material more readily available to
other libraries. This microfiche collection is now (1985) distributed by
University Microfilm, Incorporated of Ann Arbor, Michigan.

VITAL RECORDS 1841 - 1890

Births, marriages and deaths are recorded first at the town or city clerk's
offices. Since 1841, it has been mandated that a copy of each record be sent to
the State Registrar of Vital Records. Therefore, after that date, either the
town or the centralized state records may be consulted. At the local level,
prices and policies vary from town to town. At the State Vital Records Department, state-wide indexes to births, marriages and deaths greatly facilitate the
search for records. In 1983, new legislation allowed the State Vital Records
from 1841 to 1890 to be completely open for research. These records were then
transferred to the State Archives, which was moved from the State House to a new
facility at Columbia Point in September of 1985.

MASSACHUSETTS STATE ARCHIVES
Columbia Point
Dorchester, MA 02125

(Before Sept 1985, Archives
 still at State House)

Directions: Southeast expressway (Rte
93) to Columbia Road exit. Follow signs
to University of Massachusetts and State
Archives. By subway: Red line to Columbia Station (Ashmont Branch); shuttle bus
to Archives, UMass, JFK Library.

No fees. Limited staff-operated photocopying. Fees vary. 3 microfilm readers.
1 reader/printer. Holdings: Non-current records of the Commonwealth of
Massachusetts including state returns of vital records, 1841-1890, and
accompanying surname index. Certified copies of VRs $3. Lists of alien passen-
gers arriving in the Port of Boston, 1848-1891, and surname index. Federal
census records, 1840-1880, including supplemental schedules, 1850-1870, and
state census returns of 1855 and 1865. "Massachusetts Archives" collection of
colonial and revolutionary era documents, including land grants by the General
Court, military records (1643-1787) and tax valuations. Approximately one
quarter of the collection has been catalogued in a surname/town name index;
military records are indexed separately. Papers documenting the settlement of
Maine and the separation of that state from Massachusetts.

VITAL RECORDS AFTER 1890

REGISTRAR OF VITAL STATISTICS
150 Tremont Street, Room B-3
Boston, MA 02111
617-727-0110
Mon, Wed, Fri 2-4:30 p.m.
Tues, Thurs 9-11 a.m.

Facing the Common near the Tourist
Information Booth. Park under the
Common or in garages at the Government
Center (expensive!). Or take subway
to Park St. or Boylston St.

Open to researchers. No fee. Must sign book upon entering. All death records are open. For birth and marriage records, a clerk has to inspect the specific records before permission is given for the researcher to view it. Separate state-wide alphabetical indexes for births, marriages and deaths are in 5-year compilations. Staff-operated photocopying only to make certified copies. $3 per record.

****

CITIES AND TOWNS OF MASSACHUSETTS

The cities and towns listed below were taken from Historical Data relating to Counties, Cities and Towns in Massachusetts, 1966. For more detailed information, consult that work and also the list of Massachusetts Vital Records prepared by Edward Hanson in Genealogical Research in New England, Genealogical Publishing Co., 1984; pp 97-108, 113-114. Codes used for Vital Records of the various towns are:

ARNOLD ("Vital Records of Rhode Island, 1636-1850," by James N. Arnold. 21
    volumes. Available at many major libraries.)
COOKE (The "Roland H. Cooke Collection" at the Berkshire Athenaeum, Pittsfield)
CORBIN (The "Corbin Collection" at New England Historic Genealogical Society,
    Boston).
DAR (The DAR Library, Washington, D.C.).
MD (The Mayflower Descendant; journal of the Mayflower Society, available at
    many major libraries).
MSS (Manuscript or Typescript)
PMV (Miscellaneous published volumes, not part of the official series).
POS (Volumes published as part of the "official series").
REG (New England Historical and Genealogical Register).
SPT ("See parent town").
X (No V.R.s published. Inquire at the town.)

TOWN	ESTABLISHED	PARENT TOWN(S)	COUNTY	CODE
Abington	1712	Bridgewater	Plymouth	POS
Acton	1735	Concord	Middlesex	POS
Achusnet	1860	Fairhaven	Bristol	SPT
Adams	1778	----	Berkshire	COOKE
(formerly the "East Hoosuck" plantation)				
Agawam	1855	W. Springfield	Hampden	SPT
Alford	1773	Great Barrington	Berkshire	POS
Amesbury	1668	Salisbury	Essex	POS
(called "Salisbury new town" until 1668)				
Amherst	1759	Hadley	Hampshire	CORBIN
Andover	1646	----	Essex	POS
Arlington	1807	Cambridge	Middlesex	POS
(called "West Cambridge" until 1867				
Ashburnham	1765	----	Worcester	POS
(formerly the "Dorchester-Canada" plantation)				
Ashby	1767	Ashburnham, Fitchburg & Townsend	Middlesex	MSS/NEHGS

TOWN	ESTABLISHED	PARENT TOWN(S)	COUNTY	CODE
Ashfield	1765	----	Franklin	POS
(formerly "Huntstown" plantation)				
Ashland	1846	Framingham, Holliston & Hopkinton	Middlesex	SPT
Athol	1762	----	Worcester	POS
(formerly "Payquage" plantation)				
Attleboro	1694	Rehoboth	Bristol	POS
Auburn	1778	Leicester, Oxford	Worcester	POS
(called "Ward" until 1837)		Sutton & Worcester		
Avon	1888	Stoughton	Norfolk	SPT
Ayer	1871	Groton & Shirley	Middlesex	SPT
Barnstable	1638	----	Barnstable	MD/PMV
Barre	1753	Rutland	Worcester	POS
(called "Rutland District" until 1774, "Hutchinson" until 1776)				
Becket	1765	----	Berkshire	POS
(formerly No. 4 plantation)				
Bedford	1729	Billerica & Concord	Middlesex	POS
Belchertown	1761	----	Hampshire	CORBIN
(formerly "Cold Spring" plantation)				
Bellingham	1719	Dedham, Mendon, Wrentham	Norfolk	POS
Belmont	1859	Waltham, Watertown, W. Cambridge (now Arlington)	Middlesex	SPT
Berkley	1735	Dighton & Taunton	Bristol	MSS/NEHGS
Berlin	1784	Bolton & Marlborough	Worcester	PMV
Bernardston	1762	----	Franklin	CORBIN
(formerly "Falltown" plantation)				
Beverly	1668	Salem	Essex	POS
Billerica	1655	----	Middlesex	POS
Blackstone	1845	Mendon	Worcester	SPT
Blandford	1741	----	Hampden	CORBIN
(formerly "Suffield Equivalent," commonly called "Glasgow")				
Bolton	1738	Lancaster	Worcester	POS
Boston	1630	----	Suffolk	PMV

(V.R.s for Boston are in Reports of the Record Commissioners of Boston, volumes 9, 24, 28 & 30 - also published separately by Gen. Pub. of Baltimore; V.R.s from ca 1800-1848 are at Room 201, City Hall, Boston. Researchers may use the collection, including original records from the colonial period for Boston and the several annex towns, for a fee of $4 per hour, 9-5, Mon-Fri. Certified copies $5. Boston Church Record transcripts are also in Room 201.)

TOWN	ESTABLISHED	PARENT TOWN(S)	COUNTY	CODE
Bourne	1884	Sandwich	Barnstable	SPT
Boxborough	1783	Harvard, Littleton, Stow	Middlesex	POS
Boxford	!694	----	Essex	POS
Boylston	1786	Shrewsbury	Worcester	POS
Bradford	1675	----	Essex	POS
(annexed to Haverhill 1897)				
Braintree	1640	Boston (Mt. Woollaston)	Norfolk	PMV
Brewster	1803	Harwich	Barnstable	POS
Bridgewater	1656	----	Plymouth	POS
Brighton	1817	Cambridge	Suffolk	X/SPT
(annexed to Boston 1874)				
Brimfield	1714	----	Hampden	POS
Brockton	1821	Bridgewater	Plymouth	POS
(called "North Bridgewater" until 1874)				

TOWN	ESTABLISHED	PARENT TOWN(S)	COUNTY	CODE
Brookfield	1673	----	Worcester	POS
Brookline	1705	Boston	Norfolk	POS
Buckland	1779	"No-town plantation" & Charlemont	Franklin	POS
(V.R.s bound with Colrain & Montague)				
Burlington	1799	Woburn	Middlesex	POS
Cambridge	1631	----	Middlesex	POS
(called "Newe Towne" until 1636)				
Canton	1797	Stoughton	Norfolk	POS
Carlisle	1780	Acton, Billerica, Chelmsford, Concord	Middlesex	POS
Carver	1790	Plympton	Plymouth	POS
Charlemont	1765	----	Franklin	POS
Charlestown	1630	----	Suffolk	PMV
(annexed to Boston 1874)				
(Volume I of V.R.s published by NEHGS, 1985. Vol II in preparation)				
(See also Wyman, Genealogies & Estates of Charlestown)				
Charlton	1754	Oxford	Worcester	POS
Chatham	1712	----	Barnstable	MD
(formerly called "Manamoit Village")				
Chelmsford	1655	----	Middlesex	POS
Chelsea	1739	Boston	Suffolk	POS
(formerly called "Winnissimet," "Rumney Marsh," "Pullin Point")				
Cheshire	1793	Adams, Lanesborough, Windsor, New Ashford District	Berkshire	X
Chester	1765	----	Hampden	POS
(called "Murrayfield" until 1783)				
Chesterfield	1762	----	Hampshire	CORBIN
(formerly "New Hingham" plantation)				
Chicopee	1848	Springfield	Hampden	SPT
Chilmark	1694	----	Dukes	POS
Clarksburg	1798	----	Berkshire	X
Clinton	1850	Lancaster	Worcester	SPT
Cohasset	1770	Hingham	Norfolk	POS
Colrain	1761	----	Franklin	POS
(V.R.s bound with Buckland and Montague)				
Concord	1635	----	Middlesex	POS
(formerly called "Musketequid")				
Conway	1767	Deerfield	Franklin	POS
Cummington	1779	"No. 5" plantation	Hampshire	PMV
Dalton	1784	----	Berkshire	POS
(formerly called "Ashuelet Equivalent")				
Dana	1801	Greenwich, Hardwick & Petersham	Worcester	POS
(annexed to Petersham 1927)				
Danvers	1752	Salem	Essex	POS
(formerly called "Salem Village and Middle Parishes")				
Dartmouth	1652	----	Bristol	POS
(formerly called "Acushena," "Ponagansett" & "Coaksett")				
Dedham	1636	----	Norfolk	POS
Deerfield	1677	----	Franklin	POS
Dennis	1793	Yarmouth	Barnstable	MD
Dighton	1712	Taunton	Bristol	CORBIN

TOWN	ESTABLISHED	PARENT TOWN(S)	COUNTY	CODE
Dorchester	1630	----	Suffolk	PMV
(Dorchester was annexed to Boston in 1870)				
(V.R.s for Dorchester are in Reports of the Record Commissioners of Boston, Vols. 21 & 36)				
Douglas	1746	----	Worcester	POS
(formerly called "New Sherbourn")				
Dover	1784	Dedham	Norfolk	POS
Dracut	1702	----	Middlesex	POS
Dudley	1732	Oxford	Worcester	POS
Dunstable	1673	----	Middlesex	POS
Duxbury	1637	----	Plymouth	POS
E. Bridgewater	1823	Bridgewater	Plymouth	POS
E. Brookfield	1920	Brookfield	Worcester	SPT
E. Longmeadow	1894	Longmeadow	Hampden	SPT
Eastham	1646	----	Barnstable	MD/PMV
(called "Nawsett" until 1651)				
Easthampton	1785	Northampton, Southampton	Hampshire	CORBIN
Easton	1725	Norton	Bristol	MSS/NEHGS
Edgartown	1671	----	Dukes	POS
(formerly known as "Great Harbour")				
Egremont	1760	----	Berkshire	X
Enfield	1816	Belchertown, Greenwich	Hampshire	CORBIN
(annexed to Belchertown, New Salem, Pelham & Ware in 1938)				
Erving	1838	----	Franklin	X
Essex	1819	Ipswich	Essex	POS
Everett	1870	Malden	Middlesex	SPT
Fairhaven	1812	New Bedford	Bristol	X
Fall River	1803	Freetown	Bristol	DAR
(called "Troy" from 1804 to 1834)				
Falmouth	1694	----	Barnstable	PMV
(V.R.s in "Genealogical Advertiser")				
Fitchburg	1764	Lunenburg	Worcester	PMV
Florida	1805	"Barnardstone's Grant" & part of "Bullock's Grant"	Berkshire	X
Foxborough	1778	Stoughton, Walpole, Wrentham & Stoughtonham (now Sharon)	Norfolk	POS
Framingham	1675	----	Middlesex	POS
Franklin	1778	Wrentham	Norfolk	POS
Freetown	1683	----	Bristol	MSS/NEHGS
(V.R.s in "Genealogical Advertiser")				
Gardner	1785	Ashburnham, Templeton, Westminster & Winchendon	Worcester	POS
Gay Head	1855	----	Dukes	
Georgetown	1838	Rowley	Essex	POS
Gil	1793	Greenfield	Franklin	POS
Gloucester	1642	----	Essex	POS
(formerly called "Cape Ann")				
Goshen	1781	Chesterfield	Hampshire	CORBIN
Gosnold	1864	Chilmark	Dukes	SPT
Grafton	1735	----	Worcester	POS
(formerly "Hassanamisco" plantation)				
Granby	1768	South Hadley	Hampshire	CORBIN
Granville	1754		Hampden	POS

TOWN	ESTABLISHED	PARENT TOWN(S)	COUNTY	CODE
Gt. Barrington	1761	Sheffield	Berkshire	POS
Greenfield	1753	Deerfield	Franklin	POS
Greenwich	1754	----	Worcester	MSS/NEHGS /DAR
(formerly "Quabin" plantation)				
(annexed 1938 to Hardwick, New Salem, Petersham & Ware)				
Groton	1655	----	Middlesex	POS
Groveland	1850	Bradford	Essex	SPT
Hadley	1661	----	Hampshire	MSS/NEHGS /CORBIN
(formerly the "New Plantation")				
Halifax	1734	Middleborough, Pembroke & Plympton	Plymouth	POS
Hamilton	1793	Ipswich	Essex	POS
Hampden	1878	Wilbraham	Hampden	SPT
Hancock	1776	----	Berkshire	CORBIN
(formerly "Jericho" plantation)				
Hanover	1727	Abington & Scituate	Plymouth	POS
Hanson	1820	Pembroke	Plymouth	POS
Hardwick	1739	----	Worcester	POS
(formerly "Lambstown" plantation)				
Harvard	1732	Groton, Lancaster, Stow	Worcester	POS
Harwich	1694	----	Barnstable	MD/PMV
(formerly "Satuckett")				
Hatfield	1670	Hadley	Hampshire	CORBIN/NEHGS
Haverhill	1641	----	Essex	POS
Hawley	1792	----	Franklin	CORBIN
(formerly "No. 7" plantation)				
Heath	1785	Charlemont	Franklin	POS
Hingham	1635	----	Plymouth	MSS/NEHGS
(called "Barecove" until 1635)				
Hinsdale	1804	Patridgefield (now Peru) & Dalton	Berkshire	POS
Holbrook	1872	Randolph	Norfolk	SPT
Holden	1741	Worcester	Worcester	POS
Holland	1783	South Brimfield (now Wales)	Hampden	X
Holliston	1724	Sherborn	Middlesex	POS
Holyoke	1850	W. Springfield	Hampden	SPT
Hopedale	1886	Milford	Worcester	SPT
Hopkinton	1715	----	Middlesex	POS
(formerly called "Moguncoy")				
Hubbardston	1767	Rutland	Worcester	POS
Hudson	1866	Marlborough & Stow	Middlesex	SPT
Hull	1644	----	Plymouth	POS
Huntington	1773	Murrayfield	Hampshire	X
(called "Norwich" until 1855)				
Ipswich	1634	----	Essex	POS
(formerly "Aggawam")				
Kingston	1726	Plymouth	Plymouth	POS
Lakeville	1853	Middleborough	Plymouth	SPT
Lancaster	1653	----	Worcester	POS
Lanesborough	1765	----	Berkshire	PMV/CORBIN
(formerly "New Framingham" plantation)				
Lawrence	1847	Andover & Methuen	Essex	POS
Lee	1777	Great Barrington	Berkshire	POS

TOWN	ESTABLISHED	PARENT TOWN(S)	COUNTY	CODE
Leicester	1714	----	Worcester	POS
Lenox	1767	Richmont (now Richmond)	Berkshire	COOKE
Leominster	1740	Lancaster	Worcester	POS
Leverett	1774	Sunderland	Franklin	CORBIN
Lexington	1713	Cambridge	Middlesex	POS
Leyden	1784	Bernardston	Franklin	X
Lincoln	1754	Concord, Lexington, Weston	Middlesex	POS
Littleton (formerly "Nashoba")	1715	----	Middlesex	POS
Longmeadow	1783	Springfield (Longmeadow)	Hampden	REG
Lowell	1826	Chelmsford	Middlesex	POS
Ludlow	1774	Springfield	Hampden	NEHGS
Lunenburg	1728	"Turkey Hills" & land belonging to Woburn, Dorchester & Boardman's Farm	Worcester	PMV
Lynn (called "Saugust" until 1637)	1635	----	Essex	POS
Lynnfield	1782	Lynn	Essex	POS
Malden	1649	----	Middlesex	POS
Manchester	1645	Salem	Essex	POS
Mansfield	1770	Norton	Bristol	POS
Marblehead	1633	----	Essex	POS/PMV
Marion	1852	Rochester	Plymouth	SPT
Marlborough	1660	----	Middlesex	POS
Marshfield (formerly "Green's Harbour" & Rexhame)	1640	----	Plymouth	PMV/MD
Mashpee	1763	----	Barnstable	X
Mattapoisett	1857	Rochester	Plymouth	SPT
Maynard	1871	Stow & Sudbury	Middlesex	SPT
Medfield	1650	Dedham	Norfolk	POS
Medford	1630	----	Middlesex	POS
Medway	1713	Medfield	Norfolk	POS
Melrose	1850	Malden	Middlesex	SPT
Mendon	1667	----	Worcester	POS
Merrimac	1876	Amesbury	Essex	SPT
Methuen	1725	Haverhill	Essex	POS
Middleborough (formerly "Namassackett")	1669	----	Plymouth	MD/PMV
Middlefield	1783	Becket, Chester, Partridgefield (now Peru) Washington, Worthington & "Prescott's Grants"	Hampshire	POS
Middleton	1728	Andover, Boxford, Salem & Topsfield	Essex	POS
Milford	1780	Mendon	Worcester	POS
Millbury	1813	Sutton	Worcester	POS
Millis	1885	Medway	Norfolk	SPT
Millville	1916	Blackstone	Worcester	SPT
Milton	1662	Dorchester	Norfolk	POS
Monroe	1822	Rowe and "The Gore"	Franklin	X
Monson	1760	Brimfield	Hampden	CORBIN
Montague (V.R.s bound with Buckland and Colrain)	1754	Sunderland	Franklin	POS
Monterey	1847	Tyringham	Berkshire	SPT

TOWN	ESTABLISHED	PARENT TOWN(S)	COUNTY	CODE
Montgomery	1780	Westfield, Norwich (now Huntington) & Southampton	Hampden	POS
Mt. Washington	1779	----	Berkshire	X
(formerly "Tauconnuck Mt." plantation)				
Nahant	1853	Lynn	Essex	SPT
Nantucket	1687	----	Nantucket	POS
(called "Sherburn" until 1713, "Tuckannock" until 1795)				
Natick	1650	----	Middlesex	POS
Needham	1711	Dedham	Norfolk	REG/NEHGS
New Ashford	1781	----	Berkshire	POS
New Bedford	1787	Dartmouth	Bristol	POS
New Braintree	1751	Hardwick & Brookfield	Worcester	POS
New Marlborough	1759	----	Berkshire	COOKE
New Salem	1753	----	Franklin	POS
Newbury	1635	----	Essex	POS
(formerly "Wessacucon")				
Newburyport	1764	Newbury	Essex	POS
Newton	1691	----	Middlesex	POS
(formerly "Cambridge Village" or "New Cambridge")				
Norfolk	1870	Franklin, Medway, Walpole & Wrentham	Norfolk	SPT
North Adams	1878	Adams	Berkshire	SPT
North Andover	1855	Andover	Essex	SPT
N. Attleborough	1887	Attleborough	Bristol	SPT
N. Brookfield	1812	Brookfield	Worcester	X
N. Reading	1853	Reading	Middlesex	SPT
Northampton	1656	----	Hampshire	CORBIN
Northborough	1766	Westborough	Worcester	POS
Northbridge	1772	Uxbridge	Worcester	POS
Northfield	1714	----	Franklin	CORBIN
(formerly "Squakeag" plantation)				
Norton	1710	Taunton	Bristol	POS
Norwell	1849	Scituate	Plymouth	SPT
(called "South Scituate" until 1888)				
Norwood	1872	Dedham & Walpole	Norfolk	SPT
Oak Bluffs	1880	Edgartown	Dukes	SPT
(called "Cottage City" until 1907)				
Oakham	1762	Rutland	Worcester	POS
Orange	1783	Athol, Royalston, Warwick & "Ervingshire tract"	Franklin	X
Orleans	1797	Eastham	Barnstable	MD/PMV
(published with Eastham)				
Otis	1773	Tyringham Equivalent	Berkshire	POS
(called "Loudon" until 1810)				
Oxford	1693	----	Worcester	POS
Palmer	1752	----	Hampden	POS
(formerly called "The Elbows" plantation)				
Paxton	1765	Leicester & Rutland	Worcester	CORBIN
Peabody	1855	Danvers	Essex	SPT
(called "South Danvers" until 1868)				
Pelham	1743	----	Hampshire	POS
(formerly "New Lisburn" tract)				
Pembroke	1712	Duxbury	Plymouth	POS

TOWN	ESTABLISHED	PARENT TOWN(S)	COUNTY	CODE
Pepperell	1753	Groton	Middlesex	PMV
Peru	1771	----	Berkshire	POS
(called "Partridgefield" until 1806)				
Petersham	1754	----	Worcester	POS
(formerly "Nichewoag" plantation)				
Phillipston	1786	Athol & Templeton	Worcester	POS
(called "Gerry" until 1814)				
Pittsfield	1761	----	Berkshire	COOKE
(formerly "Pontoosuck" plantation)				
Plainfield	1785	Cummington	Hampshire	COOKE
Plainville	1905	Wrentham	Norfolk	SPT
Plymouth	1620	----	Plymouth	PMV/MD
Plympton	1707	Plymouth	Plymouth	POS
Prescott	1822	Pelham & New Salem	Worcester	NEHGS
(annexed 1938 to Pelham & New Salem)				
Princeton	1759	Rutland	Worcester	POS
Provincetown	1727	----	Barnstable	MD
(formerly precinct of Cape Cod)				
Quincy	1792	Braintree & Dorchester	Norfolk	NEHGS
Randolph	1793	Braintree	Norfolk	NEHGS
Raynham	1731	Taunton	Bristol	REG
Reading	1644	Lynn	Middlesex	POS
Rehoboth	1645	----	Bristol	POS
(formerly called "Seacunk")				
Revere	1846	Chelsea	Suffolk	SPT
(called "North Chelsea" until 1871)				
Richmond	1765	----	Berkshire	POS
(called "Richmont" until 1785)				
Rochester	1686	----	Plymouth	POS
(also called "Scippicam")				
Rockland	1874	Abington	Plymouth	SPT
Rockport	1840	Gloucester	Essex	POS
Rowe	1785	----	Franklin	CORBIN
(formerly called "Myrefield")				
Rowley	1639	----	Essex	POS
Roxbury	1630	----	Suffolk	POS
(annexed to Boston 1868)				
Royalston	1765	----	Worcester	POS
(formerly "Royalshire" tract)				
Russell	1792	Westfield & Montgomery	Hampshire	CORBIN
Rutland	1714	----	Worcester	POS
(formerly "Naquag" tract)				
Salem	1630	----	Essex	POS
Salisbury	1639	----	Essex	POS
(called "Colechester" until 1640)				
Sandisfield	1762	----	Berkshire	POS
(formerly "No. 3" plantation)				
Sandwich	1638	----	Bristol	MD/PMV
Saugus	1815	Lynn	Essex	POS
Savoy	1797	----	Berkshire	CORBIN
Scituate	1633	----	Plymouth	POS
Seekonk	1812	Rehoboth	Bristol	Arnold Papers

TOWN	ESTABLISHED	PARENT TOWN(S)	COUNTY	CODE
Sharon	1765	Stoughton	Norfolk	POS
(called "Stoughtonham" until 1783)				
Sheffield	1733	----	Berkshire	COOKE/NEHGS
Shelburne	1768	Deerfield	Franklin	POS
Sherborn	1674	----	Middlesex	POS
Shirley	1753	Groton	Middlesex	POS
Shrewsbury	1720	----	Worcester	POS
Shutesbury	1761	----	Franklin	CORBIN/Index only
(formerly "Roadtown" plantation)				
Somerset	1790	Swansea	Bristol	X
Somerville	1842	Charlestown	Middlesex	SPT
S. Hadley	1753	Hadley	Hampshire	CORBIN
Southampton	1753	Northampton	Hampshire	CORBIN
Southborough	1727	Marlborough	Worcester	POS
Southbridge	1816	Charlton, Dudley, Sturbridge	Worcester	PMV
Southwick	1770	Westfield	Hampden	X
Spencer	1753	Leicester	Worcester	POS
Springfield	1641	----	Hampden	REG/CORBIN
Sterling	1781	Lancaster	Worcester	PMV
Stockbridge	1739	----	Berkshire	NEHGS
(formerly "Indian town" plantation)				
Stoneham	1725	Charlestown	Middlesex	POS
Stoughton	1726	Dorchester	Norfolk	PMV
Stow	1683	----	Middlesex	POS
(formerly (Pompositticut" plantation)				
Sturbridge	1738	"New Medfield" tract	Worcester	POS
Sudbury	1639	----	Middlesex	POS
Sunderland	1714	----	Franklin	CORBIN
(called "Swampfield" until 1718)				
Sutton	1714	----	Worcester	POS
Swampscott	1852	Lynn	Essex	SPT
Swansea	1667	Rehoboth	Bristol	POS
(called "Wannamoisett" until 1668)				
Taunton	1639	----	Bristol	POS
(formerly called "Cohannett")				
Templeton	1762	----	Worcester	POS
(formerly "Narragansett No. 6" plantation)				
Tewksbury	1734	Billerica	Middlesex	POS
Tisbury	1671	----	Dukes	POS
(formerly "Middletowne")				
Tolland	1810	Granville	Hampden	X
Topsfield	1648	Ipswich	Essex	POS/PMV
Townsend	1732	----	Middlesex	X
(formerly part of "Turkey Hills")				
Truro	1709	----	Barnstable	POS
(formerly "Pawmett" tract)				
Tyngsboro	1789	Dunstable	Middlesex	POS
Tyringham	1762	----	Berkshire	POS
(formerly "No. 1" plantation)				
Upton	1735	Hopkinton, Mendon, Sutton & Uxbridge	Worcester	POS
Uxbridge	1727	Mendon	Worcester	POS

MASSACHUSETTS

TOWN	ESTABLISHED	PARENT TOWN(S)	COUNTY	CODE
Wakefield	1812	Reading	Middlesex	POS
(called "South Reading" until 1868)				
Wales	1762	Brimfield	Hampden	CORBIN
(called "South Brimfield" until 1828)				
Walpole	1724	Dedham	Norfolk	POS
Waltham	1738	Watertown	Middlesex	POS
Ware	1761	----	Hampshire	CORBIN
(formerly "Ware River Parish")				
Wareham	1739	Rochester & "Agawam" plantation	Plymouth	MD/PMV
Warren	1742	Brimfield, Brookfield, Kingsfield	Worcester	POS
(called "Western" until 1834)				
Warwick	1763	----	Franklin	CORBIN
(formerly "Roxbury Canada" plantation)				
Washington	1777	----	Berkshire	POS
(formerly "Hartwood" plantation)				
Watertown	1630	----	Middlesex	PMV
Wayland	1780	Sudbury	Middlesex	POS
(called "East Sudbury" until 1835)				
Webster	1832	Dudley & Oxford	Worcester	PMV
Wellesley	1881	Needham	Norfolk	SPT
Wellfleet	1763	Eastham	Barnstable	MSS/NEHGS
Wendell	1781	Shutesbury, Ervingshire	Franklin	X
Wenham	1643	----	Essex	POS
W. Boylston	1808	Boylston, Holden, Sterling	Worcester	POS
W. Bridgewater	1822	Bridgewater	Plymouth	POS
W. Brookfield	1848	Brookfield	Worcester	SPT
W. Newbury	1819	Newbury	Essex	POS
(called "Parsons" until 1820)				
W. Springfield	1774	Springfield	Hampden	POS
W. Stockbridge	1774	Stockbridge	Berkshire	POS
W. Tisbury	1892	Tisbury	Dukes	SPT
Westborough	1717	Marlborough	Worcester	POS
Westfield	1669	Springfield	Hampden	CORBIN
Westford	1729	Chelmsford	Middlesex	POS
Westhampton	1778	Northampton	Hampshire	CORBIN
Westminster	1759	----	Worcester	POS
(formerly "Narragansett No. 2...)				
Weston	1713	Watertown	Middlesex	POS
Westport	1787	Dartmouth	Bristol	POS
Westwood	1897	Dedham	Norfolk	SPT
Weymouth	1635	----	Norfolk	POS
(formerly "Wessaguscus")				
Whately	1771	Hatfield	Franklin	
(V.R.s abstracted in Whately 1771-1971: A New England Portrait, by Ena M. Crane; Family Records, by Paul F. Field. Northampton, MA, 1972.)				
Whitman	1875	Abington, E. Bridgewater	Plymouth	SPT
(called "South Abington" until 1886)				
Wilbraham	1763	Springfield	Hampden	CORBIN/DAR
Williamsburg	1771	Hatfield	Franklin	X

MASSACHUSETTS

TOWN	ESTABLISHED	PARENT TOWN(S)	COUNTY	CODE
Williamstown (formerly "West Hoosuck" plantation)	1765	----	Berkshire	POS
Wilmington	1730	Reading, Woburn	Middlesex	POS
Winchendon (formerly "Ipswich Canada" plantation)	1764	----	Worcester	POS
Winchester	1850	Medford, Woburn, W. Cambridge (now Arlington)	Middlesex	SPT
Windsor (called "Gageborough" until 1778)	1771	----	Berkshire	POS
Winthrop (called "North Chelsea" until 1852)	1846	Chelsea	Suffolk	SPT
Woburn (formerly "Charlestowne Village")	1642	----	Middlesex	PMV
Worcester (formerly "Quansigamond" plantation)	1684	----	Worcester	POS
Worthington (formerly "No. 3" plantation)	1768	----	Hampshire	POS
Wrentham (formerly "Wollonopaug")	1673	----	Norfolk	POS
Yarmouth (formerly "Mattacheeset")	1639	----	Barnstable	PMV

****

CENSUS RECORDS - FEDERAL

NATIONAL ARCHIVES - BOSTON BRANCH
380 Trapelo Road
Waltham, MA 02154
617-647-8100
Mon-Fri 8-4:30

From Route 128, take Trapelo Road exit (east). Low brick building on right side, two and three-quarter miles from Route 128.

Open to researchers. No fee. Approximately 20 microfilm readers. Self-service for microfilm. Films are arranged on open shelves. Holdings include microfilms of all U.S. Censuses from 1790 to 1910 for every state in the U.S., but only small parts of 1890 which was mostly destroyed by fire. Many printed indexes to censuses are here also, from 1790 to 1850. These printed indexes (also available at NEHGS and other major libraries) save the researcher many hours of searching. The indexes, which list only the heads of families, indicate the page of the census on which a given name occurs. The censuses themselves are not in alphabetical order. A "Soundex index" on microfilm to the 1880, 1900 and 1910 censuses is an index to heads of households also. (The 1910 Soundex index is available for only 23 states.) A card for the head of a household will list every person residing in that household, but there will not be separate index cards for every person. It should also be noted that the 1880 Soundex index is only a partial index. It includes only those households which had someone ten years of age or younger residing in the household. On the other hand, the 1900 and 1910 Soundex index includes all households.

The Records center also has microfilm copies of Revolutionary War pension and bounty land warrant application files and compiled military service records, as well as indexes to these records. The Center also has microfilm copies of passenger lists for the ports of Boston, 1891-1921, New Bedford, Massachusetts, 1902-1919, and Portland, Maine, 1820-1868. Among the original records in the Center are naturalization records for the Federal courts in Maine, Massachusetts, Vermont, Rhode Island and Connecticut. The Maine, Massachusetts and Vermont naturalization records include name indexes while those for Connecticut and Rhode Island do not. You must contact the Clerks of the latter two courts for information from the indexes. Copies of originals may be obtained from Washington, D.C.

INTERLIBRARY LOAN FOR FEDERAL CENSUS RECORDS ON MICROFILM

Census Records on microfilm may be borrowed from at least two sources:

CENSUS MICROFILM RENTAL PROGRAM   Charge: $3.25 per film.
P.O. Box 2940   Be sure to specify the reel number.
Hyattsville, MD 20784

(Reel numbers may be ascertained from three booklets available from the National Archives Trust Fund Board, Washington D.C.: "Federal Population Censuses, 1790-1890," "1900 Federal Population Census" and "1910 Federal Population Census.")

THE AMERICAN GENEALOGICAL LENDING LIBRARY (AGLL) is a private lending system. For an initial fee of $30 and annual renewals of $15, individuals or institutions may borrow films, including U.S. Census, Ship Passenger Lists, Rev. War Pension and Bounty-Land-Warrant Application Files, from a 50,000 film-library. Loans are $2.50 per film to an individual, $2 to an institution. Purchases are $9 per roll to both. For further information, send a SASE to: AGLL, P.O. Box 244, Bountiful, Utah 84010.

FEDERAL CENSUS RECORDS AFTER 1910

Census records after 1910 in custody of the Bureau of Census are confidential but can be furnished to the person to whom data pertains or, if deceased, to a direct bloodline relative, member of the immediate family or surviving spouse, together with proof of death; to administrator or executor of estate, with court order of appointment; or to beneficiary with proof of such entitlement, as by will or insurance. Application forms may be obtained from:

PERSONAL CENSUS SERVICE BRANCH
BUREAU OF THE CENSUS
Pittsburg, Kansas 66762

****

CENSUS RECORDS - STATE

State Censuses for 1855 and 1865 are available at the Massachusetts State Archives. (See entry under Massachusetts - Libraries - Boston)

****

MASSACHUSETTS

PROBATE AND LAND RECORDS

In Massachusetts, all Probate and Land Records are at the county level. There are five counties which have more than one registry office. the researcher must be aware of the dates of creation of various counties and districts.

BARNSTABLE COUNTY was established in 1685 from New Plymouth Colony.

Probate Court (Barnstable County)
or Registry of Deeds   "   "
Main Street
Barnstable, MA 02630
617-362-2511
Mon-Fri 8-4:30
Directions: Rte 6 to 132.
Right to light. Left one mile
to Barnstable Village
and Courthouse

Probate records: 1686 to present;
Record books only. (Earlier records
at Plymouth.)   Deeds: 1703 to present.
Original records 1686-1827 destroyed by
fire, but many re-recorded.
Pre-1686 records are at Plymouth

BERKSHIRE COUNTY was established in 1761 from Hampshire County. Prior to 1761, deeds for the towns in Berkshire County were recorded at Springfield. Probate Records from 1761 for all of Berkshire County are at Pittsfield, but the Registries of Deeds are at three locations from 18 June 1788: The Northern District is at Adams. It includes Adams, Cheshire, Clarksburg, Florida, Hancock, Lanesborough, New Ashford, North Adams, Savoy, Williamstown, and Windsor. The Middle District is at Pittsfield. It includes Becket, Dalton, Hinsdale, Lee, Lenox, Otis, Peru, Pittsfield, Richmond, Stockbridge, Tyringham and Washington. The Southern District is at Great Barrington. It includes Alford, Egremont, Great Barrington, Monterey, Mount Washington, New Marlborough, Sandisfield, Sheffield, and West Stockbridge.

Registry of Deeds (Northern District)
65 Park Street
Adams, MA 01220
413-743-0035
Directions: Rte 7 to Rte 9 East. Rte 8 North. 12.3 miles to Court House.
2 story brick building.

Deeds: 1788-present.
(1761-1788 at Pittsfield)
(prior to 1761 at Springfield)

Registry of Deeds (Middle District)
or Probate Court (Berkshire County)
44 Bank Row
Pittsfield, MA 01201
413-443-7438 (Registry of Deeds)
413-442-6941 (Probate)
Registry of Deeds: Mon-Fri 8:30-4:30
Probate Court: Mon-Fri 8:15-4:30
Directions: Route 20 to Rte 7 & 20. 7.4 miles to Rotary. Third building
on right hand side.

Probate Records: 1767-present.
Deeds: 1761-present.
(prior to 1761 at Springfield)

Registry of Deeds (Southern District)
Great Barrington, MA 01230
413-528-0146
Directions: Rte 102 west. 11.8 miles.
Registry is in the Town Hall (a two-story
brick building).

Deeds: 1788-present.
(1761-1788 at Pittsfield)
(prior to 1761 at Springfield)

BRISTOL COUNTY was established in 1685 from New Plymouth Colony. Bristol was
the shire-town until 13 November 1746 when it was succeeded by Taunton. Probate
records are all at Taunton, but the Registries of Deeds are at three locations:
The Northern District is at Taunton. It includes Attleborough, Berkley,
Dighton, Easton, Mansfield, North Attleborough, Norton, Raynham, Rehoboth,
Seekonk, Taunton. The Southern District is at New Bedford. It includes Acush-
net, Dartmouth, Fairhaven, New Bedford, Westport. The Fall River District is at
Fall River. It includes Fall River, Freetown, Somerset, and Swansea.

Probate Court
or Registry of Deeds (Northern District)
  11 Court Street
  Taunton, MA 02780
  Mon-Fri 8:30-4:30
  617-824-4004 (Probate) 2nd floor.
  617-822-3081 (Deeds) 1st floor.
  Directions: Rte 24 south to Rte 44 west
  Turn left at Taunton Green. Red brick
  building.

Deeds: 1686-present.
(Earlier deeds at Plymouth)

Probate Records: 1687-present.
(Earlier deeds at Plymouth)

Registry of Deeds (Southern District)
  25 North 6th Street
  New Bedford, MA 02740
  Mon-Fri 8:30-5
  617-993-2603 & 2605

Deeds: 1837-present
(Earlier records at Taunton
and Plymouth)

Directions: Follow County Street South to Williams Street. Go left 2 blocks
to 6th Street. One-story yellow brick building.

Registry of Deeds (Fall River District)
  441 North Main Street
  Fall River, MA 02720
  Mon-Fri 8:30-5
  617-673-1651 & 2910

Deeds: 1686-1891 copied
records.
Deeds: 1892-present.

Directions: Rte 195 west to Exit 12. (Pleasant St.) 2 blocks. Left onto
8th St. 1 block. Left onto Bedford. 4 blocks to No. Main St. 7 blocks to
Walnut St. Two-story granite building corner of Maple Street.

DUKES COUNTY was established in 1683 under the jurisdiction of New York and was incorporated by Massachusetts Bay in 1695.

Probate Court (Dukes County)
or Registry of Deeds (Dukes County)
   Edgartown, MA 02539
   Mon-Fri 8:30-4:30
   617-627-4703 (Probate)
   617-627-4025 (Deeds)

Probate Records: 1696-present
Deeds: 1686-present

Directions: Courthouse is brick building on left of Road to Edgartown.

ESSEX COUNTY was established in 1643. The Probate Records are all at Salem, but the Registries of Deeds are at two locations: <u>The Southern District is at Salem</u>. It includes Amesbury, Beverly, Boxford, Danvers, Essex, Georgetown, Gloucester, Groveland, Hamilton, Haverhill, Ipswich, Lynn, Lynnfield, Manchester, Marblehead, Merrimac, Middleton, Nahant, Newbury, Newburyport, Peabody, Rockport, Rowley, Salem, Salisbury, Saugus, Swampscott, Topsfield, Wenham, West Newbury. <u>The Northern District is at Lawrence</u>. It includes Andover, Lawrence, Methuen, North Andover.

Registry of Deeds (Southern District)
or Probate Court (Essex County)
   32 Federal Street
   Salem, MA 01970
   Mon-Fri 8-4:30
   617-741-0201
   Directions: Rte. 128 to Rte 114 to Rte 107 to Washington St. One block Federal St. Two-story granite building. Parking lot & garage two blocks beyond.

Deeds: Ipswich Series, 1640-1694; old county of Norfolk series, 1637-1714; Salem series, 1640 to present.

Probate Records: 1643 to present.

Registry of Deeds (Northern District)
   381 Common Street
   Lawrence, MA 01840
   Mon-Fri 8:00 a.m.-5:00 p.m.
   617-683-2745 & 2746

Deeds: 1869 to present. Earlier deeds at Salem. (Essex Probates, 1635-1681 have been published in 3 vols.)

Directions: Rte 128 to Rte 93 North to Rte 495 to Rte 114 to Canal Street. Turn left. Right on Hampshire St. Right onto Common St. Three-story yellow brick building on left. Metered parking on street.

FRANKLIN COUNTY was established in 1811 from Hampshire County.

Registry of Deeds (Franklin County)
or Probate Court (Franklin County)
   425 Main Street
   Greenfield, MA 01310
   Mon-Fri 8:30 - 4:30
   413-774-7011 (Probate)
   413-772-0239 (Registry)
   Directions: Two-story red brick building at corner of Main & Hope Streets across from Post Office.

Deeds: 1663-1786 (Abstracts only)
Deeds: 1787 to present. (Earlier deeds at Springfield)

Probate Records: 1812 to (Earlier probates at Northampton)

HAMPDEN COUNTY was established in 1812 from Hampshire County. The Registry at Springfield was the Registry for the original county at Hampshire, which comprised the present county of Berkshire until 1761; the present county of Franklin until 1811; the present county of Hampden until 1812; certain towns afterward in the present county of Worcester; and the towns of Somers and Suffield now in the state of Connecticut. The Hampshire County Deeds to the time Hampden County was formed, are at Springfield, and the Hampshire County Probates, including the present Hampden County for the period before the division are at Northanmpton.

Probate Court (Hampden County)
or Registry of Deeds (Hampden County)
  50 State Street
  Springfield, MA 01103
  Mon-Fri 8:00 - 4:30
  413-781-8100
  Directions: In New Hall of Justice Building.

Probate Records: 1812 to present.
(Earlier records at Northampton)

Deeds: 1636 to present.

HAMPSHIRE COUNTY was established in 1662 from Middlesex County.

Probate Court (Hampshire County)
or Registry of Deeds (Hampshire County)
  33 King Street
  Northampton, MA 01060
  Mon-Fri 8:00 - 4:30
  413-586-8500 (Probate)
  413-584-3637 (Registry)
  Directions: Rtes 5 & 10 to Northampton Center.
Two-story gray cement building with brown trim.

Probate Records: 1660 to present.
(Earlier Records at Cambridge)

Deeds: 1812 to present.
(Earlier deeds at Springfield)

MIDDLESEX COUNTY was established in 1643. All Probate Records are at Cambridge, but the Registries of Deeds are in two locations: The Southern District is at Cambridge and includes Acton, Arlington, Ashby, Ashland, Ayer, Bedford, Belmont, Boxborough, Burlington, Cambridge, Concord, Everett, Framingham, Groton, Holliston, Hopkinton, Hudson, Lexington, Lincoln, Littleton, Malden, Marlborough, Maynard, Medford, Melrose, Natick, Newton, North Reading, Pepperell, Reading, Sherborn, Shirley, Somerville, Stoneham, Stow, Sudbury, Townsend, Wakefield, Waltham, Watertown, Wayland, Weston, Winchester and Woburn. The Northern District is at Lowell and includes Billerica, Carlisle, Chelmsford, Dracut, Dunstable, Lowell, Tewksbury, Tyngsborough, Westford, Wilmington.

Probate Court (Middlesex County)
or Registry of Deeds (Southern District)
  208 Cambridge Street
  Cambridge, MA 02141
  Mon-Fri 8 - 4
  617-494-4500
  Directions: Storrow Drive through Leverett
Circle onto O'Brien Highway to Lechmere Square. Left under elevated to Cambridge. Two blocks. Red brick building. Via MBTA: Lechmere car on Green Line from Government Center to end of line.

Probate Records: 1654-present.

Deeds: 1649 to present.
Hopkinton and Upton Deeds, 1743-1833 - 19 volumes.

76

Registry of Deeds (Northern District)
360 Gorham Street
Lowell, MA 01852   Deeds: 1855 to present.
617-458-8474 & 8475   (Earlier deeds at Cambridge)
Directions: Rte 3 North to Lowell Connector to end of Gorham Street. Turn
left. Two-story sandstone building on right.

NANTUCKET COUNTY was established in 1695. The town of Nantucket is the only
town in the county.

Probate Court (Nantucket County)
or Registry of Deeds (Nantucket County)   Probate Records: 1706-present.
Broad Street
Nantucket, MA 02554   Deeds: 1659-present.
Mon-Fri 8:30 - 4:00 (Probate)
617-228-2669 (Probate)
Mon-Fri 8:00 - 4:00 (Registry)
617-228-0454 (Registry)
Directions: Two-story building on left side of Broad Street. One-quarter
mile from ferry.

NORFOLK COUNTY. The old Norfolk County, established in 1643, comprised
Exeter, Salisbury, Hampton, Haverhill, Dover and Strawberry Banke (afterwards
Portsmouth). It was abolished in 1679. The records are at Salem. The present
Norfolk County was established in 1793 from Suffolk County.

Probate Court (Norfolk County)
or Registry of Deeds (Norfolk County)   Probate Records: 1793-present.
649 High Street   (Earlier records at Boston)
Dedham, MA 02026
Mon-Fri 8:30 - 4:30   Deeds: 1793-present.
617-326-7200 (Probate)   (Earlier deeds at Boston)
617-326-1600 (Registry)
Directions: Rte 1 south to High Street. Turn left. One-half mile to
Dedham Center. Two-story granite building on corner.

PLYMOUTH COUNTY was established in 1685 from New Plymouth Colony.

Plymouth County Commissioners' office   All of the early original
South Russell Street   Plymouth Colony records
Plymouth, MA 02360   previous to 2 June 1685
617-747-1350 ext. 10   are at the Plymouth County
                                         Commissioners' office.

Probate Family Court Dept. - Plymouth Div.
or Registry of Deeds (Plymouth County)
    Russell Street
    Plymouth, MA 02360
    617-747-0500, ext. 146 (Probate)
    617-747-1350 (Registry)
    Directions: Rte 44 South to Rte 3A
    (Court Street). One mile to Russell
    St. Turn right.

Wills: 1633-1686
Deeds: 1620-1686

Registry of Deeds has copies of
Vital Records for most towns in
Plymouth County. Also copies
of most Proprietors records.
See Ruth W. Sherman & Robert S.
Wakefield, Plymouth County
Probate Guide (1983)
NEHGS will publish Plymouth
County Probate Index in 1985.

SUFFOLK COUNTY was established in 1643.

Probate Court (Suffolk County)
or Registry of Deeds (Suffolk County)
    Old Court House
    Pemberton Square
    Boston, MA 02108
    617-725-8575
    Directions: Storrow Drive to
    Cambridge Street. Turn right onto
    Somerset. Center Plaza Parking.

Probate Records: 1636-present.
Early indexes are published.
Estates of over 50 pounds for all
Dominion of New England 1686-1689
Early Suffolk Co. wills published
Baltimore: Gen Pub. Co., 1984)

Deeds: 1639-present. Block Island
Records to 1663. Map of early
estates of Boston. (Records of
extinct cities & towns at City Hall).
First 14 volumes of Suffolk Deeds
are printed.

WORCESTER COUNTY was established in 1731 from Suffolk and Middlesex Counties. The Probate Records are all at Worcester, but the Registries of Deeds are at two locations. The Worcester District is at Worcester. It includes Athol, Auburn, Barre, Berlin, Blackstone, Bolton, Brookfield, Charlton, Clinton, Douglas, Dudley, East Brookfield, Gardner, Grafton, Hardwick, Harvard, Holden, Hopedale, Hubbardston, Lancaster, Leicester, Mendon, Milford, Millbury, Millville, New Braintree, North Brookfield, Northborough, Northbridge, Oakham, Oxford, Paxton, Petersham, Phillipstown, Princeton, Royalston, Rutland, Shrewsbury, Southborough, Southbridge, Spencer, Sterling, Sturbridge, Sutton, Templeton, Upton, Uxbridge, Warren, Webster, Westborough, West Boylston, West Brookfield, Winchendon, Worcester. The Northern District is at Fitchburg. It includes Ashburnham, Fitchburg, Leominster, Lunenberg, Westminster.

Probate Court
or Registry of Deeds (Worcester District)
2 Main Street
Worcester, MA 01608
Mon-Fri 8:30-4
617-756-2441
Directions: Mass Pike to Rte 122. North 3 miles to Rte 290. North one mile to Rte 9. West one-half mile to Lincoln Square. Around rotary to Main St. One block from Highland St. Up hill to Harvard St. Turn right. Multilevel building on right.

Probate Records: 1731-present.

Deeds: 1731-present.
(Prior to 1731, deeds for Worcester, Lancaster, Westborough, Shrewsbury, Southborough, Leicester, Rutland, & Lunenburg are at Cambridge. Deeds for Mendon, Woodstock, Oxford, Sutton and Uxbridge are at Boston. The Brookfields and parts of Southbridge, Sturbridge & Woodstock are at Springfield.)
Upton deeds, 1743-1833 are at Cambridge.

Registry of Deeds (Northern District)
84 Elm Street
Fitchburg, MA 01420
617-342-2637 & 2132 & 9641

Deeds: August 1884 to present.
(Earlier deeds at Worcester)

Directions: Rte 2 to 12 North to Rte 2A to Pritchard St. Turn right to Elm St. Turn left. Three story brick building two blocks down on right.

###

CEMETERY RECORDS

In Massachusetts there is no central depository of cemetery records. However, some printed records and some manuscript records for individual towns do exist. Also, most of the Massachusetts Vital Records to 1850 (official series) do include cemetery records. Many of the "old burying grounds" have been copied and published in journals such as "The Register," "Essex Institute Historical Collections" and the "Mayflower Descendant." Some DAR chapters have recorded cemeteries in their localities, and public libraries and historical societies often have manuscript cemetery records. The "Corbin" and "Cooke" collections at NEHGS and the Berkshire Athenaeum contain many cemetery records for towns in western Massachusetts. For more recent years, especially with larger cemeteries, record offices exist on or near the premises. These offices keep card files by name and will usually assist persons looking for a particular family name. It is always helpful to visit a cemetery since the arrangement of stones provides a clue to relationships not available elsewhere.

###

CHURCH RECORDS

Church records vary considerably with each denomination, but in general, most include baptisms, marriages, burials, confirmations, admissions and dismissals. The latter two categories can provide interesting clues when following the movements of a family. Church records are considered highly reliable - the best being kept by the Quakers and the Lutherans.

MASSACHUSETTS

The local church pastor is custodian of church records and should be the first person to consult. If early records are not at the local church, the pastor will usually know where the records are kept. If a church is defunct, records should be sought at the nearest historical society or library. Some denominations maintain archival records at their headquarters. The following religious bodies have depository collections in Massachusetts.

CATHOLIC

Catholic Church Records are under the jurisdiction of the local parishes. In recent years, however, a move has begun to centralize early records by Diocese. In Massachusetts, there are four Dioceses: Boston, Fall River, Springfield and Worcester. But only Boston has established an archives to date. This serves Eastern Massachusetts and a project to microfilm the collection is underway.

Archives of the Archdiocese of Boston
2121 Commonwealth Avenue
Brighton, MA 02135
617-254-0100
Mon-Fri 9-5 except holidays and Holy Days.

No fees. Photocopying available. Certificates prepared at $2 each. Requests by mail answered but no extensive research done. Records are arranged chronologically by Parish. Holdings: Pre-1910 baptismal and marriage records for approximately 150 Eastern Massachusetts Parishes. See James M. O'Toole, Guide to the Archives of the Archdiocese of Boston. N.Y.: Garland, 1983.

CONGREGATIONAL

The Congregational Library
14 Beacon Street
Boston, MA 02108
617-523-0470
Mon-Fri 9-4:30

Located diagonally across from the State House near the corner of Park St. Parking at Common Garage on Charles St. or MBTA to Park St. Station.

The Congregational Library was established in 1853 by the American Congregational Association. Its services are available to ministers and lay people of all denominations without fee. Books may be borrowed free of charge by mail for a 4 week loan period. Holdings: 225,000 books and pamphlets, including local church histories, town histories and theological works of five centuries, sermons, Bibles, etc. (See Worthley. An Inventory of... under Books and Articles - Massachusetts)

EPISCOPALIAN

The Diocesan Library and Archives
The Episcopal Diocese of Massachusetts
1 Joy Street
Boston, MA 02108
617-742-4720
Mon-Fri 9-5 (appointments preferred)

Joy Street runs off Beacon Street one block down from the State House toward Back Bay.

The pre-1905 parish registers of 104 open and closed parishes of the Diocese of Massachusetts are available on microfilm at the Diocesan Archives. Included are records of baptisms, marriages, burials, and communicant listings. Copies of the registers of eleven of the thirteen colonial parishes in the Diocese are located in the Diocesan Archives.

JEWISH   (See American Jewish Historical Society Library under MASSACHUSETTS - LIBRARIES - WALTHAM)

METHODIST

Boston University School of Theology Library
745 Commonwealth Avenue
Boston, MA 02215
617-353-3034

Holdings: Records of churches no longer in existence and some early records of current churches that belong to the Southern New England Conference of the United Methodist Church. Mostly Massachusetts, but some from Connecticut and Rhode Island and a very few from Maine.

QUAKER (Friends)

Records for all New England are at the Rhode Island Historical Society Library. (See entry under RHODE ISLAND - LIBRARIES - PROVIDENCE) The Essex Institute in Salem has the Salem Meeting Records on microfilm.

UNITARIAN/UNIVERSALIST

Harvard Divinity School Library
45 Francis Avenue
Cambridge, MA 02138   Off Kirkland Street. Parking permit
617-495-5770 $3 per day at Divinity School Office.
Mon-Fri 9-5 (please call ahead)   Subway: Harvard Square.

Holdings: Large collection of Unitarian and Universalist records and archives, including the Library of the Universalist Historical Society (the major repository of Universalism in the world) which was given to Harvard in 1976, the archives of the Unitarian Universalist Association, the American Unitarian Association, and the Unitarian Universalist Service Committee. The records include those for numerous closed Unitarian and Universalist churches, and a few on microfilm for churches still active. These include minute books, financial records, membership, birth, death records as well as records for related groups such as women's groups, youth groups, and Sunday schools. Some records for ministers concerning marriages, deaths, etc. Persons wishing to study the material should contact the Curator of Manuscripts at the Divinity School.

MILITARY RECORDS

Military matters in Massachusetts are well-recorded. Two major sets of bound volumes (official state publications) are important first references: Massachusetts Soldiers and Sailors of the Revolutionary War (17 volumes, plus microfilm supplement) and Massachusetts Soldiers, Sailors and Marines in the Civil War (9 volumes). There are also single published volumes for King Philip's War and other colonial wars. The D.A.R. Patriot Index should be checked as well. The original military records of colonial Massachusetts (as well as of Maine) are at the Massachusetts State Archives. (See entry under MASSACHUSETTS-LIBRARIES-BOSTON.) A microfilm copy of the "General Index to Compiled Military Service Records of Revolutionary War Soldiers" is at the National Archives - Boston Branch. (See MASSACHUSETTS - CENSUS RECORDS)

Military Records from 1 July 1781 (Militia Records) up to the Korean War time period are at the state Adjutant General's Office. Records prior to 1861 are of those that served in the Massachusetts Militia and may have been called to active duty during state emergencies.

    Commonwealth of Massachusetts - Military Division
    Adjutant General's Office
    War Records, Room 1000
    100 Cambridge Street, Boston, MA 02202. Tel: 617-727-2964.

    (See also)
    National Guard Armory
    Mass. Military History Research Institute
    143 Speen St., Natick, MA 01760   Tel: 617-651-5766
    Hours: Call before visiting.

Holdings: Early Militia (1776-1820); Massachusetts Militia Period (1820-1840); Pre-Civil War Period (1840-1860); Civil War (1861-1865); Reconstruction period after the Civil War (1866-1897); Spanish American War/Philippines Insurrection (1898-1917); World War I Period (1917-1919) including WW II State Guard Records; National Guard Records (1920-1940).

To obtain a copy of original military service records (including pension records and bounty-land warrant applications), write to:

    Military Service Branch (NNMS)
    National Archives and Records Service
    8th and Pennsylvania Avenues, NW
    Washington, D.C. 20408

They will send the proper form (NATF Form 80) which must be filled out and returned. There is a nominal fee if the search is successful.

For records of World War I, II and subsequent service, write to:

    National Pension Records Center, GSA
    (Military Records)
    9700 Page Boulevard
    St. Louis, MO 63132

Note: For a detailed account of military records of interest to genealogists, read: Val D. Greenwoods's The Researcher's Guide to American Genealogy, Chapters 21 and 22, and Guide to Genealogical Research in the National Archives (1982), Chapters 4 through 9.

****

IMMIGRATION AND NATURALIZATION RECORDS

Immigration and Naturalization records are maintained by the court in which the person was naturalized and may be obtained directly from the Clerk of Court. Records from 1906 to the present may also be obtained from the U.S. Department of Justice, Washington, D.C. or from the Federal office in each state.

Immigration and Naturalization Service
U.S. Department of Justice
JFK Federal Building, Government Center
Boston, MA 02203
617-223-0201   Mon-Fri 8-3:00

Policies: Information on naturalization will be provided for $15 per name, only if the name, date and court is known. For a copy of original document, one must apply directly to the Department of Justice Immigration and Naturalization Service in Washington, D.C. Application must be made on the proper form obtainable to the JFK Building by mail.

A card index to pre-1906 Naturalization Records for Suffolk County is in the Suffolk County Court House, Clerk of Courts Office (The Old Building). (A card index to all pre-1906 naturalization records for Massachusetts is at the Federal Archives and Records Center at Waltham.)

For further information on Immigration and Naturalization Records, see Massachusetts State Archives under MASSACHUSETTS - LIBRARIES - BOSTON. See also Federal Archives and Records Center under MASSACHUSETTS - CENSUS RECORDS.

****

LIBRARIES

There are 351 public libraries in Massachusetts. Their holdings vary greatly. The majority of them have small collections which may include items of genealogical interest. Many are open 12 hours a week or less and do not have staff to do research. For a list of all libraries, consult the American Library Directory in most large libraries to see what is available and what hours of service are offered. The libraries included here have genealogical collections worthy of note.

AMHERST - JONES LIBRARY
43 Amity Street   From corner of Rtes 9 and 16 in center
Amherst, MA 01002   of Amherst, go north to NW corner of
417-256-0246   common. Go left - just past the bank.
Mon, Tues, Wed, Thurs, Fri
9-5; Sat 10-5

Materials do not circulate. Staff photocopying .10 per page. Copies by mail $2.50 minimum, at .50 handling and .25 per page. Three microfilm readers. Genealogical material in Boltwood Room(s) under jurisdiction of Curator for Special Collections and access must be gained through his permission. Collection includes 950 published genealogies, 400 reference and general books, 6,500 books and documents of local history, mostly Massachusetts, and especially the history of the Pioneer Valley. Manuscript collection includes Lucius Boltwood papers. Microfilm segment includes local newspapers, U.S. Census for Hampshire County (all reels) through 1910, and film of the Boltwood Papers. Records of certain local churches are on deposit. Permission to use must be obtained. Current periodicals: 3 genealogical, 2 historical. Acquisitions budget: $1,490 per year.

AMHERST - UNIVERSITY OF MASSACHUSETTS/AMHERST LIBRARY
Amherst, MA 01003   On UMass/Amherst Campus. Parking
413-545-0150   nearby at Campus Center Garage.
Hours vary with academic year.

No fees. Open stacks. Massachusetts residents may have borrowing privileges. Photocopying: .10 per page. Microfilm photocopying: .20 per print. Microfiche photocopying: .10 per print. 18 microfilm readers; 13 microfiche readers; 2 micro-opaque readers. Sources available on microformat: U.S. Census schedules: 1790-1830 for all states; 1840-1880 for Massachusetts, selected New England states, NY, Ohio, Virginia; 1900 Massachusetts; extensive collection of newspaper backfiles; early Suffolk County deeds, probates, court records; a portion of early Massachusetts Archives collection; Hampshire County probates to 1820; U.S. City Directories to 1860; Town records for Middlesex County through 1830 plus a few other town records; Howes Brothers photographic collection, ca. 1882-1907; a complete set of Massachusetts Harbor and Land Commission Town boundary atlases, 1898-1916. Other sources include: an extensive collection of New England local history; a few printed genealogies. In Special Collections are land ownership maps and atlases of New England, New York and New Jersey ca. 1865 - ca. 1920.

BOSTON - BOSTON PUBLIC LIBRARY
Copley Square   Storrow Drive to Beacon St. to Exeter
Boston, MA 02117   St. Left on Exeter 4 blocks. Parking
617-536-5400   gargage on Exeter beyond Library.
Mon-Fri 9-9; Sat 9-6   By subway, take Copley Square exit.

Non-residents of Massachusetts may obtain a monthly courtesy card by showing I.D. Massachusetts residents apply for regular card free of charge. Holdings: The Social Sciences Reference Department maintains a separate catalog of family genealogies which include analytics and vertical file material not presented in the main public card catalog, and a rather unique index of family coats-of-arms (chiefly from the British Isles); a very comprehensive collection of histories of the British Isles. The Microtext Department (first floor old building) includes Colonial and Massachusetts newspapers from 1704, indexes to obituaries contained in selected Boston newspapers, 1704-1840, and from 1875 on; an index to the "Boston Evening Transcript" Genealogical Column from 1901-1935, including micro-cards of the actual columns; the "Hartford Times" genealogical columns, and an extensive microfiche collection of city directories for Boston and other major U.S. Cities, late 1700s to 1901. Probate Court records for Suffolk County, Massachusetts through 1852 and for Middlesex County through 1871, with indexes for both counties through 1909. "Passenger Lists" on microfilm include arrivals at Boston from 1820-1918, with indexing for 1848-1891, 1899-1916; partial arrivals at miscellaneous Gulf and Atlantic ports from 1820-1874, with indexing; all available US Censuses for the New England states from 1790, and the Veterans census of 1890; microfilm publications of the Massachusetts Historical Society; a growing collection of town records for Middlesex County, Boston City Records and Documents; the Local History and Genealogical Collection; American Loyalist Claims; Colonial Office records for American and West Indies, Massachusetts and New England; records of the American Colonization Society. The Microtext Department has 20 microfilm readers, 4 microprint readers, 3 positive printing photocopy machines for microfilm and microfiche, one positive printing photocopy machine for opaque microforms.

BOSTON - THE MASSACHUSETTS HISTORICAL SOCIETY LIBRARY
    1154 Boylston Street   Storrow Drive to Kenmore Sq./Park St.
    Boston, MA 02215   exit. Up ramp. Left at lights on
    617-536-1608 or 1609   Boylston St. Library 1st bldg on right.
    Mon-Fri 9-4:45   Subway stop: Auditorium.

No fees. Donations appreciated. Staff-operated photocopying. Collection includes manuscripts, rare books on history of Massachusetts, New England and United States, The Annie Haven Thwing Collection of early Boston residents. Special indexes. Winthrop, Adams, Saltonstall, Minot and Paine papers. 300,000 items. Many maps. No genealogical resources, per se.

BOSTON - THE MASSACHUSETTS STATE ARCHIVES (See page 60)

BOSTON - THE NEW ENGLAND HISTORIC GENEALOGICAL SOCIETY LIBRARY
    101 Newbury Street   Storrow Drive to Beacon Street to
    Boston, MA 02116   Arlington Street to Newbury Street.
    617-536-5740   Parking garage on Clarendon Street.
    Tues - Sat 9-4:45   Subway exit: Copley Sguare.

Fees: $10 per day for non-members of the Society. $40 annual membership; $60 family; $10 student. Air-conditioned. Well-trained staff. Self-service photocopying $.25 per page. Change available. No food on premises. Restaurants nearby. Two microfilm readers; two fiche readers. One reader/printer. Collection: Largest holdings of family genealogies and local histories in New England. Complete holdings of many major Genealogical Journals and of the American Genealogical and Biographical Index (AGBI). Largest genealogical manuscript collection in Massachusetts. Many special indexes. 300,000 items, including the 1798 Direct Tax for Massachusetts and Maine, the Hancock papers, and the Torrey Collection of New England Marriages prior to 1700. The Greenlaw Index (a card-index to names found in genealogies and town histories received at NEHGS from 1900 to 1940) was published in two bound volumes in 1979 and is now available at many major libraries. Also, the John H. Cook collection of continental European genealogical material, and a set of the Mormon International Genealogical Index.

BOSTON - THE STATE LIBRARY OF MASSACHUSETTS

341 State House
Beacon Street
Boston, MA 02133
Mon-Fri 8:45-5

Storrow Drive to Beacon Street.
Parking under Common
Subway exit: Park Street Station

No fees. Coin-op photocopier .15 per page. Change available. Requests by mail (maximum 15 prints) .15 per page or $1 minimum. Requests by mail require prepayment. Microfilm copies .50 each. Collection: Index to all Boston newspapers, N.Y. Times and Wall St. Journal. Collection of town and county histories strongest in state. File of Massachusetts city and county atlases and roll maps. Telephone directories complete for Massachusetts, 50 state capitals and other major cities. Some foreign cities. Current and historic Directories for Mass. cities & towns back to 1789.

BROCKTON - BROCKTON PUBLIC LIBRARY

304 Main Street
Brockton, MA 02401
617-587-2515
Mon-Thur 9-9; Fri, Sat 9-5

From Rte 24 take Rte 123 East (Belmont St.) into center of Brockton. Turn right on Main Street. Library is one block down on left at corner of White Ave. and Main St. next to YMCA.

Photocopying self-service .10 per page. Two microfilm readers, one reader/printer. No fees, but modest donations and SASE's appreciated to obtain copies of obituaries and brief information requests. No inter-library loan or circulation of materials from historical room. Patron must "sign in" at reference desk to use locked genealogy and historical room. The David E. Crosby Historical room holds over 3000 volumes of Massachusetts town histories, New England genealogies and Brockton histories. Brockton Poll Tax Books from 1896, City Directories from 1869, "Mayflower Descendant" Vols. 1-34; "NEHGS Register" and "Massachusetts Vital Records to 1850" are in the room. Microfilm of Brockton and North Bridgewater newspapers from 1850 can be obtained at the circulation desk.

CAMBRIDGE - THE CAMBRIDGE PUBLIC LIBRARY

449 Broadway
Cambridge, MA 02138
617-498-9080
Mon-Fri 9-9; Sat 9-5 (closed Saturdays July & August)

Near Harvard Square.
On-street parking near library.

No fees. Photocopying .10 per page. Microfilm and microfiche readers and reader/printer. No Interlibrary Loan. Collection: Relatively large collection of New England and local history and genealogy.

DEERFIELD - THE MEMORIAL LIBRARIES

P.O. Box 53   Rte 5 to Old Deerfield. West on
Memorial Street   Memorial Street. Large brick building
Deerfield, MA 01342   on right. Limited parking adjacent
413-774-5581 Ext. 125   to building.

No fees. Photocopying .10 per page. Microfilm, microfiche readers. Largely closed stacks. The building houses two distinct libraries: The Pocumtuck Valley Memorial Association Library, and the Henry N. Flynt Library of Historic Deerfield, Inc. The latter supports the activities of Historic Deerfield, and has relatively little of genealogical interest. The PVMA Library has sizeable collections of family papers (more than 200), diaries and account books. Hampshire County probates and town and census records on microfilm. Area cemetery transcriptions, published and mss. genealogies, local history materials and indices. Collections of George Sheldon. Tries to cover Franklin County extensively. The Memorial Libraries in Deerfield provide the only full-time historical collection freely available to the public in Franklin County, and one of the few such organizations in western Massachusetts. The staff is small and not permitted to undertake projects tracing individual lines, but makes every effort to answer all inquiries.

HAVERHILL - HAVERHILL PUBLIC LIBRARY

Corner of Main & Summer Sts.   Rte 495 to Rte 97 to Main Street.
Haverhill, MA 01830   Go up hill to Library at corner of
617-373-1586 & 1587   Main & Summer Streets.
Mon-Thurs 9-9; Fri, Sat 9-5:30 Free parking lot.
(Hours change frequently, so call
ahead, especially for summer & Sunday hrs)

The Special Collections of the Haverhill Public Library are housed in air-conditioned, carpeted rooms with ample seating and several professional staff members available. Photocopying is done by staff at .25 per page, available the following day. The Collections are all non-circulating. Included are the Haverhill History Collection (4,000 volumes) and the Pecker Genealogy Collection (2,500 volumes of family histories, with emphasis on lower Merrimack Valley and Essex County; complete Massachusetts Vital Records to 1850; the American Genealogical-Biographical Index, and complete sets of the "NEHGS Register" and "Essex Institute Historical Collections;" the Pecker Local History Collection (500 volumes of town histories of New England and some other areas of U.S.; numerous volumes of military history of the Revolutionary and Civil Wars).

LYNN - LYNN PUBLIC LIBRARY

North Common Street
Lynn, MA 01902
617-595-0567
Mon & Tues, 12-9; Wed & Thurs
9-6; Fri & Sat 9-5
(call ahead for summer hours)

Rte 129 to 107 (Western Ave.) to
Franklin St. to North Common St.
Limited metered parking in front.
Ample side-street parking.

No fees. Coin-operated photocopying .10 per page. Reference collection does
not circulate. Closed stacks. Patron must request titles and wait 5-10 minutes
for staff retrieval. 3 microfilm readers, 1 fiche reader, 1 reader/printer at
twenty-five cents per copy. Holdings: Extensive collection of family genealogies and town histories. All early Lynn newspapers on microfilm. Most Massachusetts Vital Records to 1850. "Boston Transcript" genealogy column with card
index. Lynn collection including scrapbooks of newspaper clippings. Reference
assistance on premises and via mail and phone.

LYNNFIELD - LYNNFIELD PUBLIC LIBRARY

18 Summer Street
Lynnfield, MA 01940
617-334-5411
Mon-Thurs, 9-9; Fri, Sat 9-5
Sun 2-5 (Closed Sat & Sun
Memorial Day to Labor Day)

Rte 128 to exit 33. West 3 miles to
Lynnfield Center. Library faces village
green. Large white wooden building with
front portico. Ample free parking.

No fees. Photocopying machine .10 per page first 20 copies. Additional copies
five cents. 2 microfilm readers, 2 microfiche readers, 1 fiche reader/printer,
2 portable fiche readers that circulate. Library is headquarters for the Essex
Society of Genealogists. Maintains genealogical charts and books for sale, and
circulates copies of taped lectures on genealogy. Holdings: approximately 2,000
volumes of genealogies and town histories for New England states plus Nova
Scotia and other provinces of eastern Canada. 20 genealogical periodicals
subscribed to in addition to retrospective collections of Essex County genealogical journals. Microfilm census records for Essex County for 1850 through
1910. A significant microfiche collection includes 2,000 family histories, a
complete set of Massachusetts Vital Records to 1850, City Directories for Essex
County, a complete run of the New York Genealogical & Biographical Record as
well as selected sources for North Carolina and Virginia. An every-name card
index of the 1850 census for Essex County was prepared by the Essex Society of
Genealogists. The manuscript "Dana Sweetser Collection" of local genealogy.

NEW BEDFORD - NEW BEDFORD FREE PUBLIC LIBRARY

613 Pleasant Street (3rd floor)
New Bedford, MA 02740
617-999-6291 & 6292
Mon-Sat 9-5

On street parking difficult. Two
municipal parking garages within
walking distance.

No fees. Two photocopying machines, .15 per copy. Six microfilm readers. Two
reader/printers, .25 per copy. Coin-operated typewriter available. Interlibrary loan of microfilms of post-1850 newspapers and some duplicate books.
Materials do not circulate. Holdings: Bristol, Plymouth, Barnstable, Nantucket

& Dukes Counties in Massachusetts and Tiverton and Little Compton, R.I. Also French-Canadian and Acadian material. Some Portuguese and Cape Verdean material. Town histories, vital records, etc. for the rest of Massachusetts and New England. New Bedford Customs House records, including about 7,000 crew lists and shipping articles, indexed by names of crew members of whaleships. Index to seamen's protection papers (citizenship papers). New Bedford vital records: births & marriages to 1890, deaths to 1968. Alphabetical listing of death and marriage notices in the New Bedford Mercury, 1807-1874. Index to obituaries in the New Bedford Standard-Times, 1969 to present. Federal censuses for Southeastern Massachusetts, 1790 to 1910. Immigration lists for the port of New Bedford, 1826 to 1942, indexed by name of immigrant, 1902-1954. The Pardon Gray Seabury Collection of manuscripts relating to Freetown, Fall River, Tiverton and Little Compton. The genealogical notes of Emma Pierce and of Elisha Leonard on Southeastern Massachusetts families.

NEWBURYPORT - NEWBURYPORT PUBLIC LIBRARY

94 State Street
Newburyport, MA 01950
617-465-4031
Tues-Thurs 9-8, Fri & Sat 9-5
(Summer: Mon-Thurs 9-8;
 Fri 9-5)

Rte 95 to Newburyport exit, Rte 113-East, left at Green St. to Merrimac St., right to State St. The Library is on the right on the upper end of State St. Large brick building. No parking.

The Genealogy and Local History Collection is housed in the climate-controlled Hamilton Room. The room will accommodate up to eight people. The room is run by volunteers under the direction of our reference librarian. No fees. Photocopying available at .10 per copy. One microfiche/microfilm reader/printer. Most Mass. Vital Records to 1850. Microfilm collection includes tax and town records for Newburyport, the Corbin Collection, the "New England Historical and Genealogical Register", Newburyport City Directories, and census microfilm for 1870-1910. Newburyport history collection includes over 4000 books, pamphlets, photographs, maps and broadsides. During the summer the room is open 10-4 Monday through Friday. Winter hours vary. Researchers are advised to call for hours.

NORTHAMPTON - FORBES LIBRARY

2 West Street
Northampton, MA 01060
413-584-8399
Mon-Thurs 9-9; Fri, Sat 9-5

From center of Northampton, west on Rte 9 one-half mile to Rte 66, which is West Street.

No fees. Photocopying machine .10 per copy. Two microfilm readers. One microfiche reader. One reader/printer .15 per copy. Holdings: Good but limited collection of genealogies and local histories. Originals and microfilm of Judd manuscripts, principally on Hampshire County families. Microfilm of Hampshire County probate and many Hampshire County town records. Coolidge collection on 2nd floor includes material on Coolidge family.

PITTSFIELD - BERKSHIRE ATHENAEUM - LOCAL HISTORY AND LITERATURE SERVICES

1 Wendell Avenue
Pittsfield, MA 01202
413-442-1559
Mon, Wed, Fri, Sat   10-5
Tues, Thurs   10-9
(Summer hours the same except Sat 10-1)

Located near Park Square, the heart of Pittsfield. On Rte 7 north heading towards Williamstown. (Take Lee exit from Mass. Turnpike. Follow Rte 7.) Free parking.

No fees. Two photocopying machines .15 per page first 10 pages, .10 thereafter. Four microfilm readers, 2 microfiche readers, one reader/printer .25 per page. The library will perform research as requested by mail and telephone within the limits of time and staffing. Minimum charge of $1 for copies of materials. The library actively encourages researchers to deposit copies of their research for the Family History File and published genealogy collection. No Interlibrary Loan. Holdings: Emphasis is placed on Berkshire County local history and genealogy, with excellent coverage for all New England states and New York State. Types of material range from published sermons to town annual reports, with special emphasis on town histories and genealogies of local families. The collection also contains much general genealogical reference material, such as the American Genealogical and Biographical Index (AGBI) and microfilm of the complete "Corbin Collection." Special collections include (1) The "Rollin H. Cooke Collection" of 18th & 19th century church and cemetery records for all towns in Berkshire County as well as surrounding communities in Western Massachusetts, New York, Vermont & Connecticut. (2) "The William Bradford Browne Collection" consisting of research notes and collected information by eminent local historians and genealogists. The Collection concentrates on Northern Berkshire communities and families. (3) "Elmer Shepard Collection" containing research notes and vital records of families throughout Western Massachusetts and other New England States. The bulk of the collection is on 3 X 5 cards.

SALEM - ESSEX INSTITUTE LIBRARY

132-134 Essex Street
Salem, MA 01970
617-744-3390
Mon-Fri 9-4:30

Rte 107 to Essex Street. Parking in new garage corner of Essex and Liberty Streets.

Fee: $2.00 per day for non-member use of library. Staff-operated photocopying twenty-five cents per page. Microfilm reader/printer available. Trained librarian on duty. Holdings: Probably the largest collection of Essex County genealogical and historical material available. Large manuscript collection. Growing microfilm collection of newspapers and manuscripts. (See also entry under MASSACHUSETTS - SOCIETIES.)

SPRINGFIELD - SPRINGFIELD CITY LIBRARY - GENEALOGY AND LOCAL HISTORY DEPARTMENT

220 State Street
Springfield, MA 01103
413-739-3871, Ext. 230
Mon, Tues, Thurs, Fri,
Sat 10:30-5, Wed 1-9

Take State Street exit from I-91. Parking available across from Library, or behind Library on Edwards St. and Quadrangle.

No fees. Photocopying .10 per page (for mail requests add postage). One microfilm reader, one microfiche reader, one microcard reader. No interlibrary loans. Telephone and mail requests honored. Holdings: Extensive collection for Springfield 1636-date including 22,000 photographs, maps, atlases, 280 feet of Vertical File material, over 1,600 linear feet of local history archives and manuscripts. Springfield City Directories 1845-present. Springfield Families 1636-1850. Springfield V. R.s 1636-1850. Springfield Newspapers 1788-present. Early settlement V.R.s for Pioneer Valley settlements 1638-1806 Pynchon Record Book. Official V.R. Series for Massachusetts. Holbrook Microfiche V. R. Series. Corbin microfilm collection. Cemetery records for most Hampden County towns and many other localities for Western Massachusetts. Very large French Canadian genealogy collection (collection guide available - $3.50) including major sets of Drouin, Tanguay, Charbonneau, Talbot, Langlois, and Bergeron. Printed census indexes 1800-1850 for New England, New York and Pennsylvania. U.S. Census for Massachusetts 1790-1910. Massachusetts State Census for 1855 and 1865. Large and growing Irish genealogy and heraldry collection including O'Casey set for Counties Cork and Kerry. Large collection of individual family genealogies for New England and Eastern Canada. Growing collection of ethnic reference material. One hundred and forty different titles of genealogical periodicals. Individualized attention given to beginners. Over thirty volunteers now assisting staff in answering mail and specialized requests.

WALTHAM - <u>AMERICAN</u> <u>JEWISH</u> <u>HISTORICAL</u> <u>SOCIETY</u> LIBRARY
2 Thornton Road   On the campus of Brandeis University
Waltham, MA 02154   Rte 128 to Rte 20 East (Weston St.).
617-891-8110   Take right onto Summit Ave. Right
Mon-Thurs 11-4; Fri 9:30-2   onto Thornton Road.

No admission fee. Staff-operated photocopying .25 per page. For substantial copying $10 per hour. Microfilm reader. (Reader/printer available at Brandeis.) Mail inquiries answered promptly. Holdings: Several hundred individual family histories and genealogies, many unavailable elsewhere; histories of individual Jewish communities, synagogues, and communal groups; several specific indexes, including a card index to 19th century Jewish periodicals (all of which the Society has as originals and on microfilm), a manuscript index to articles of American interest which appeared in European periodicals, and an index to articles of Jewish interest in American non-Jewish newspapers published before 1850; and manuscripts numbering over 500 collections, including that of the Hebrew Immigration Aid Society of Boston containing individual arrival records, arranged alphabetically, for immigrants arriving in Boston or Providence between 1882 and 1929, and incomplete chronological lists of ship arrivals and ship's passenger lists between 1904 and 1953; also the collection of the Mayor's Court, Naturalization, Insolvent Debtors, and Incorporation Papers of New York City (consisting of microfilm and bound photocopies of court records now in the New York City Hall of Records; the first three contain pre-1860 materials; the Incorporation Papers deal with all Jewish or Jewish-related organizations incorporated in New York City between 1848 and 1920. All are fully indexed). The Society also has over 300 catalogued manuscript collections dealing with individuals or families.

WESTON - BOSTON STAKE BRANCH GENEALOGICAL LIBRARY
The Church of Jesus Christ of Latter-day Saints
150 Brown Street   Rte 128 to Exit 51 (Rte 30) (South Ave.).
Weston, MA 02193   Library is in the LDS Church on the left,
617-235-9892   3.2 miles west of Rte 128, 1/4 mile
Tues 7-9; Thurs 9-3, 7-9; beyond Pope John XXIII Seminary.
Sat 9-4.

No admission fee. Ten microfilm readers. (For policies, see Nashua, N.H. Stake under NEW HAMPSHIRE - LIBRARIES - NASHUA)

WORCESTER - AMERICAN ANTIQUARIAN SOCIETY LIBRARY
185 Salisbury Street   Rte 290 to Exit 17 to Belmont St.,
Worcester, MA 01609   Lincoln Square & Salisbury St.
617-755-5221   Library is at corner of Park Ave. &
Mon-Fri 9-5   Salisbury St. Parking at rear.

Open without charge to all qualified adults, following an interview. Staff-operated photocopying .15 per copy, only for approved materials. Limited number of copies. (Write for complete policies and prices.) Minimum mail order $4.50. Facilities: Coat rack and lockers provided near main entrance. Coin-op telephone. Reader's lounge, but no facilities for dining. Closed stacks. Materials do not circulate. No Interlibrary Loan. Holdings: Three million books, pamphlets, broadsides, manuscripts, prints, maps, directories, newspapers. The largest single collection of printed source material relating to the history, literature and culture of the first 250 years of what is now the United States. Specializes in the printed record of the American experience prior to 1877. Files of 18th and 19th century newspapers the finest anywhere. Extensive collection of family histories and local history.

****

SOCIETIES

BERKSHIRE FAMILY HISTORY ASSOCIATION
Box 1437
Pittsfield, MA 01201
413-442-1559 Ext. Local History Department, for information about BFHA.

Founded 1979 to research, promote and encourage the study of family history and genealogy. Dues: $8 per year individual. $10 family. $4 students. Monthly meetings at the Berkshire Athenaeum Auditorium, Sept. through May. Publication: "The Berkshire Genealogist" free with membership. First issue 1978. All back issues available.

ESSEX INSTITUTE
132-134 Essex Street
Salem, MA 01970
617-744-3390

Founded in 1848 through a merger of the Essex County Historical Society and the Essex County Natural History Society. It is one of the oldest and largest privately-endowed historical societies in the United States. The original Essex

County Court Records are deposited here. Dues: $20 individual, $30 family, $15 Senior Citizen, $50 sustaining, $100 benefactor, $100 corporate sponsor, $300 corporate patron. Meetings: Annual Spring Meeting. Lectures, Exhibits. Museum of 39,000 objects. Library: (See entry under MASSACHUSETTS - LIBRARIES - SALEM). Publications: "Essex Institute Historical Collections," published quarterly from 1859 to the present. First 20 years have been published in 20 bound volumes. There are also published bound indexes through volume 105. The Institute has also published many and varied books, pamphlets and bulletins, including 8 volumes of the Records and Files of Quarterly Courts of Essex County (1636-1686).

ESSEX SOCIETY OF GENEALOGISTS
C/O Lynnfield Public Library
18 Summer Street
Lynnfield, MA 01940
617-334-5411

Founded in 1975 as a chapter of the Massachusetts Society of Genealogists. Became an independent Society in January 1981. Membership 600 (not restricted to Essex County). Purpose: "to encourage individuals to research their family history, to instruct beginners in methods and sources of research, to maintain a library of current and retrospective sources in Genealogy, to provide speakers of high caliber at monthly meetings, to provide an interchange of information and ideas in an atmosphere of camaraderie and mutual sharing, to maintain files and indexes, to plan projects of lasting value to genealogists." Dues: $8 per year single (as of June 1985 - will go up to $10 in 1986). $10 family (June 1985) Membership includes subscription to "The Essex Genealogist," a quarterly of 50-60 pages per issue. Meetings: monthly September through May, the 3rd Saturday of the month unless otherwise announced. Meetings held at the Old Meeting House, at the Centre Congregational Church or at the Lynnfield Public Library. Publications: "The Essex Genealogist" (TEG). Subscription: $7 per year (June 1985) or free with membership. Queries and articles accepted. "Newsletter of the Essex Society of Genealogists" quarterly, free with membership. Project: An every-name card file to the 1850 U.S. Census for Essex County. Now completed. Named "The Stallard File."

GENERAL SOCIETY OF MAYFLOWER DESCENDANTS
Four Winslow Street
Plymouth, MA 02360
617-746-3188

Founded 1897. 22,000 members. 50 state groups plus Washington, D.C., and Royal Canadian. Persons descended from a passenger on the Mayflower on the voyage which terminated at Plymouth, Massachusetts, December, 1620. Conducts research into descendants of Mayflower Pilgrims through 5th generation. Members join state chapters which then contribute an "assessment" to the General Society. Research Department established to assist bona fide applicants retrieve documentation from within Society files. Fee: $25. Meetings: Triennial - usually at Plymouth. Publications: "Mayflower Quarterly;" Mayflower Families through Five Generations (three volumes published to date); Mayflower Ancestral Index (1981).

THE IRISH ANCESTRAL RESEARCH ASSOCIATION ("TIARA")
P.O. Box 619
Sudbury, MA 01776

Founded: 1982. Dues: $8.50 per year individual, $12.75 per year for a family membership. Monthly meetings, second Friday of each month at 7:30 P.M., from January through December at Pope John XXIII Seminary, Route 30, Weston, Mass. A non-denominational organization established to provide educational programs and exchange information relating to Irish genealogical research, both Catholic and Protestant, in Dublin, Belfast, and North America. Does not do research for others. Monthly meetings Sept. through June. Publish bi-monthly Newsletter with queries. Brochure available.

MASSACHUSETTS SOCIETY OF GENEALOGISTS, INC.
P.O. Box 215
Ashland, MA 01721

Founded in 1975. Semi-autonomous chapters in Bristol, Franklin, Hampden, Middlesex and Worcester Counties. Individuals may join either at a county chapter, or, if out-of-state, at the state office. Membership includes subscription to "MASSOG", free Queries, participation in the Ancestor Service, unlimited use of the MSOG Library Collection in the Waltham Public Library, and a Membership List. Annual meeting in geographic center of State. Chapters have monthly or semi-monthly meetings. Dues: $10 single, $15 family. Publication: MASSOG, a quarterly. Single back issues $3.50. Limited advertising accepted. Write for details.

MASSACHUSETTS SOCIETY OF MAYFLOWER DESCENDANTS
101 Newbury Street
Boston, MA 02116   Executive Secretary: Shirley Robinson
617-266-1624   Pizziferri

Founded 1896 "to perpetuate to a remote posterity the memory of our Pilgrim Fathers. To maintain and defend the principle of civil and religious liberty as set forth in the Compact of the Mayflower..." Membership limited to applicants who can document their line of descent from one of the 23 proven passengers of the Mayflower. Dues: $20 per year includes subscription to the "Mayflower Quarterly," a publication of the General Society. Meetings: Three per year - the Annual Meeting in the Spring, Peregrination to Plymouth in June, and Compact Day Celebration in November. Publication: "The Mayflower Descendant", published biannually (quarterly beginning January 1986). Began publication 1985; continuation of old magazine of same name. $10/year subscription not included in Mass. Mayflower Society membership.

NEW ENGLAND HISTORIC GENEALOGICAL SOCIETY
101 Newbury Street   (See also entry under MASSACHUSETTS -
Boston, MA 02116   LIBRARIES - BOSTON)

Founded 1845. Dues: $40 per year includes subscription to "The New England Historical and Genealogical Register," a quarterly; and "Nexus," a newsletter. Membership open to all. Currently 7,000 members. Membership includes free use of library, access to bookstacks, and a lending library of more than 30,000 volumes (3-book limit per loan). Lectures by top genealogists in the country provided at the Society monthly throughout the winter season. Publications: Many and varied. List available from the Society.

THE PILGRIM SOCIETY
75 Court Street
Plymouth, MA 02360

Founded 1820 "to perpetuate the memory of the virtues, the enterprise, and the unparalleled sufferings of the First Settlers of New England who landed at that place on December 21st, 1620." Membership includes free admission to Pilgrim Hall Museum, free paperback publications of the Society, the use of the Society's library of 12,000 volumes, manuscripts, and rare books, a 10% discount on purchases over $10 in the Gift Shop, invitations to many lectures, Annual Dinner on Forefathers' Day, held since 1769, free Pilgrim Society Note series of informal papers delivered to the Society, consultation services in the area of historic preservation. Publications: "Pilgrim Society Newsletter," "Pilgrim Society Note Series," and paperback publications. Note: The Pilgrim Hall Museum has Plymouth County Court Record Books from 1686-1859.

WESTERN MASSACHUSETTS GENEALOGICAL SOCIETY, INC.
P.O. Box 206   Contact person: Joyce Holbrook
Forest Park Station
Springfield, MA 01108

Founded 1972 to provide programs of interest and help to genealogists and for the exchange of genealogical information and materials. Dues: $5 individuals. $7 family. Payable in September. Meetings the 1st Monday of each month at the Genealogy/Local History Department of the Springfield City Library at 220 State Street, Springfield, MA 01103. Publication: "The American Elm," free with membership. Queries accepted as space allows.

****

BOOKS AND ARTICLES

Barlow, Claude W., New England Genealogy: a research guide with special emphasis on Massachusetts and Connecticut. (1976)

Bowen, Richard LeBaron, Massachusetts Records: A Handbook for Genealogists, Historians, Lawyers, and other Researchers. (Rehoboth, 1957)

Dodge, Winifred Lovering Holman, (Revised by Florence and Rachel E. Barclay), "Massachusetts," in The American Society of Genealogists, Genealogical Research: Methods and Sources, Rev. ed. (Washington, D.C., 1980, I:139-49).

Hanson, Edward W. and Homer Vincent Rutherford, "Genealogical Research in Massachusetts: a Survey and Bibliographical Guide," in New England Historical and Genealogical Register, July, 1981, and in Genealogical Research in New England, Genealogical Publishing Co., 1984).

Flagg, Charles A., A Guide to Massachusetts Local History (1907).

Haskell, John D., ed. Massachusetts: A Bibliography of Its History (Boston, 1976)

Hindus, Michael S., The Records of the Massachusetts Superior Court and Its Predecessors: an Inventory and Guide. Judicial Records Committee (Boston, 1977).

Secretary of the Commonwealth, Historical Data Relating to Counties, Cities and Towns in Massachusetts (revised ed., 1975).

Worthley, Harold Field, An Inventory of the Records of the Particular (Congregational) Churches of Massachusetts Gathered 1620-1805 (Harvard Theological Studies, XXV). (Cambridge, 1970).

Wright, Carroll D., Report on the Custody and Condition of the Public Records of Parishes, Towns, and Counties (Boston, 1889).

In addition to the above sources, one should always consult the major genealogical magazines for information on Massachusetts families and towns. The guides to this literature are: Donald L. Jacobus's 3-volume Index to Genealogical Periodicals and the annual Genealogical Periodicals Index (GPAI). Among the major journals to be consulted are the New England Historical and Genealogical Register and The American Genealogist. The New York Genealogical and Biographical Record also contains considerable material on Massachusetts families. For Essex County, one should consult the Essex Antiquarian and the Essex Institute Historical Collections, and the various magazines published early in the century by Eben Putnam. For Plymouth County and Cape Cod one should see the Mayflower Descendant and the Genealogical Advertiser (also published in a bound volume by Genealogical Publishing Co., Inc. of Baltimore, Maryland). For additional lists of recommended reading for family research in Massachusetts, see the lists appended to Gilbert Doane's Searching for Your Ancestors, Noel C. Stevenson's Search and Research, and others.

****

NEW HAMPSHIRE

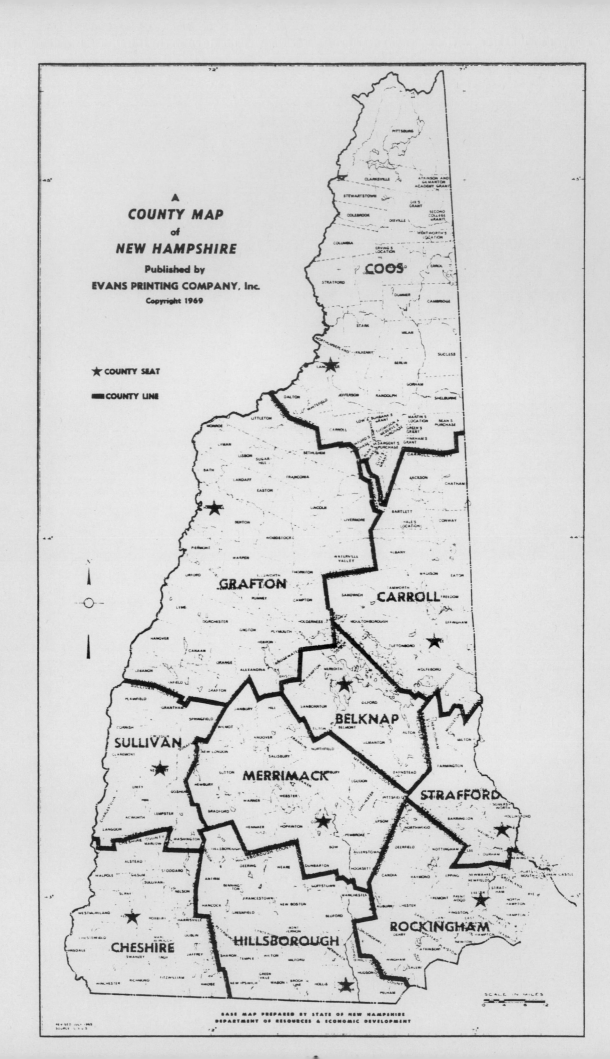

A
COUNTY MAP
of
NEW HAMPSHIRE
Published by
EVANS PRINTING COMPANY, Inc.
Copyright 1969

★ COUNTY SEAT
▬▬ COUNTY LINE

COOS

GRAFTON

CARROLL

BELKNAP

SULLIVAN

MERRIMACK

STRAFFORD

CHESHIRE

HILLSBOROUGH

ROCKINGHAM

SCALE IN MILES
0 4 8

BASE MAP PREPARED BY STATE OF NEW HAMPSHIRE
DEPARTMENT OF RESOURCES & ECONOMIC DEVELOPMENT

NEW HAMPSHIRE

With settlements at Rye and Dover in 1623, New Hampshire ranks among the oldest states in New England. Through the first half of the eighteenth century settlements were confined to the coastal region and the area around Nashua, and growth was slow. From 1642 to 1679 and from 1690 to 1692 New Hampshire was governed by Massachusetts. Under the term of Governor Benning Wentworth (1741-1767) many townships were granted in what is now Vermont and settlement of the inland portion of the colony proceeded rapidly after the French and Indian Wars. In 1764 the Connecticut River was established as New Hampshire's western boundary. The province was divided into five counties in 1769. In 1776 a provisional constitution was adopted, and in 1788 New Hampshire became the ninth state. The nineteenth century saw the settlement of the northern part of the state and the growth of mill towns such as Manchester and Nashua with the coming of the Industrial Revolution. Beginning about the time of the Civil War, large numbers of French-speaking Canadians from Quebec began to settle in New Hampshire, joining the predominantly Yankee and Scotch-Irish ethnic mix. Today the French Canadians make up about a quarter of the state's population. The Irish make up another large ethnic group.

As in Massachusetts, vital records in New Hampshire are kept by towns and land and probate records by counties. For those doing genealogical research in the pre-Revolutionary era they will find that almost all necessary records are available in Concord at the State Historical Society, the State Library, the State Records and Archives Center, or at the Department of Vital Statistics.

****

VITAL RECORDS

Each town and city clerk maintains the official record for all births, marriages and deaths. Copies are sent to the Bureau of Vital Records. Town records are not always indexed. The New Hampshire State Library has a name index to the early town records, but not every town is included and the last date is frequently 1835.

STATE OF NEW HAMPSHIRE
BUREAU OF VITAL RECORDS AND HEALTH STATISITCS
Hazen Drive   Rte 93 to exit 14. East on Rte
Concord, NH 03301   202 (Loudon Road) 1/2 mile. Turn
603-271-2561   left at traffic light at sign for
Mon-Fri 8:30-4:15   N.H. State Office Park. Follow
                                     signs to Health & Welfare Bldg.

The Vital Records room is staffed by volunteers from the New Hampshire Society of Genealogists. The volunteers retrieve all the records and explain rules and policies. The vital records are closed for the day if volunteers are not there. Fees: .50 for non-certified copies; $3 for certified. Two microfilm readers. Photocopies will be supplied by mail at $3 per search. A search fee of from $3 to $12 may be levied if exact date of event is not known - and depending on how many sections of records must be searched. <u>Holdings</u>: Birth records prior to 1901; Death, Marriage, Divorces prior to 1938. To see later records, one must demonstrate a "Direct and Tangible" interest. Note: After 1902, the Town Reports for individual towns usually list births, marriages and deaths for that town.

****

The list of New Hampshire towns below is taken from <u>New Hampshire Towns</u>, by Elmer Hunt. The first date given is the incorporation or grant date (from <u>New Hampshire State Papers</u>, Vol. 39. The second date represents the adoption of the present town name and is taken from Hunt. These books should be consulted for complete details of settlements and settlers. Codes for counties are:

BELKN (Belknap)   COOS (Coos)   MERR (Merrimack)
CARR (Carroll)   GRAF (Grafton)   ROCK (Rockingham)
CHESH (Cheshire)   HILLS (Hillsborough) STRAF (Strafford)
                                       SULL (Sullivan)

TOWN (OR INCORPORATED)	GRANTED	NAMED	COUNTY
Acworth (formerly Burnet)	1735/6	1766	SULLIVAN
Albany (formerly Burton)	1833		GRAF/STRAF/CARR
Alexandria	1753	1753	GRAFTON
Allenstown	1722	1721	MERRIMACK
Alstead (formerly No 4 & Newton)	1735/6	1763	CHESHIRE
Alton (formerly New Durham Gore)	1796	1796	STRAF/BELKN
Amherst (formerly Narragansett No 3)	1728	1760	HILLSBOROUGH
Andover (formerly Emerystown)	1751	1779	HILLS/MERR
Antrim (formerly Cumberland)	1777	1777	HILLSBOROUGH
Ashland (from Holderness)	1868	1868	GRAFTON
Atkinson (from Plaistow)	1767	1767	ROCKINGHAM
Atkinson and Gilmanton Grant (unincorporated)			COOS
Auburn (from Chester)	1845	1845	ROCKINGHAM
Barnstead	1727	1727	SRAF/BELKN
Barrington	1722	1722	STRAFFORD
Bartlett	1790	1790	GRAF/COOS/CARR
Bath	1761	1761	GRAFTON
Bean's Grant unincorp'd			COOS
Bean's Purchase "			COOS
Bedford (formerly Narragansett No 5)	1733/4	1730	HILLSBOROUGH
Belmont (formerly Upper Gilmanton)	1859	1869	BELKNAP
Bennington (from Hancock, Greenfield & Deering)	1842	1842	HILLSBOROUGH
Benton (formerly Coventry)	1764	1839	GRAFTON
Berlin (formerly Maynesborough)	1771	1829	GRAF/COOS
Bethlehem	1774	1799	GRAFTON
Boscawen (formerly Contoocook)	1732	1760	HILLS/MERR
Bow	1727	1727	ROCK/MERR
Bradford (formerly New Bradford & Bradfordton)	1735/6	1787	HILLS/MERR
Brentwood (from Exeter)	1744	1741	ROCKINGHAM
Bridgewater (from New Chester)	1788	1788	GRAFTON
Bristol (from Hill & Bridgewater)	1819	1819	GRAFTON
Brookfield (from Middleton)	1794	1794	STRAF/CARR
Brookline	1769	1798	HILLSBOROUGH
Cambridge unincorporated			Coos
Campton	1761	1761	STRAF/GRAF
Canaan	1761	1761	GRAFTON
Candia (from Chester)	1763	1763	ROCKINGHAM
Canterbury	1727	1727	ROCK/MERR
Carroll (formerly Bretton Woods)	1772	1832	GRAF/COOS
Center Harbor (from New Hampton)	1797	1797	STRAF/BELKN

TOWN (OR INCORPORATED)	GRANTED	NAMED	COUNTY
Chandler's Purchase	1835		COOS
Charlestown	1735	1753	CHESH/SULL
Chatham	1767	1767	GRAF/COOS/ STRAF/CARR
Chester	1720	1722	ROCKINGHAM
Chesterfield (formerly No 1)	1735	1752	CHESHIRE
Chichester	1727	1727	ROCK/MERR
Claremont	1764	1764	CHESH/SULL
Clarksville (formerly Dartmouth College Grant)	1792	1853	GRAF/COOS
Colebrook (formerly Dryden)	1762	1770	GRAF/COOS
Columbia (formerly Preston & Cockburntown)	1762	1811	GRAF/COOS
Concord (formerly Penacook & Rumford)	1659	1765	ROCK/MERR
Conway	1765	1765	GRAF/STRAF/ CARR
Cornish	1763	1763	CHESH/SULL
Crawford's Purchase & Crawford Notch		1834	COOS
Croyden	1763	1763	CHESHIRE
Cutt's Grant unincorp'd			COOS
Dalton (from Littleton)	1784	1784	GRAF/COOS
Danbury (from Alexandria)	1795	1795	GRAF/MERR
Danville (from Kingston)	1760	1760	ROCKINGHAM
Deerfield (from Nottingham)	1766	1766	ROCKINGHAM
Deering	1774	1774	HILLSBOROUGH
Derry (from Londonderry)	1827	1827	ROCKINGHAM
Dixville unincorporated			COOS
Dorchester	1761	1761	GRAFTON
Dover		1623	STRAFFORD
Dublin (formerly Monadnock)	1749	1771	CHESHIRE
Dummer	1773	1773	GRAF/COOS
Dunbarton (formerly Gorhamstown & Starkstown)	1735	1752	HILLS/MERR
Durham (formerly Dover Parish)	1732	1732	STRAFFORD
East Kingston (from Kingston)	1738	1738	ROCKINGHAM
Easton (from Landaff)	1876	1867	GRAFTON
Eaton	1766	1760	STRAF/CARR
Effingham	1749	1749	STRAF/CARR
Ellsworth (formerly Trecothick)	1769	1802	GRAFTON
Enfield	1761	1761	GRAFTON
Epping (from Exeter)	1741/2	1741	ROCKINGHAM
Epsom	1727	1727	ROCK/MERR
Errol	1774	1774	GRAF/COOS
Erving's Grant unincorp'd			COOS
Exeter		1638	ROCKINGHAM
Farmington (from Rochester)	1798	1798	STRAFFORD
Fitzwilliam (formerly Monadnock No 4)	1752	1773	CHESHIRE
Francestown	1772	1772	HILLSBOROUGH
Franconia (formerly Indian Head & Morristown)	1764	1782	GRAFTON
Franklin (formerly Pemigewasset)	1828	1828	MERRIMACK
Freedom (formerly North Effingham)	1831	1831	STRAF/CARR
Fremont (from Exeter) (formerly Poplin)	1764	1854	ROCKINGHAM
Gilford (from "Gunstock Parish" of Gilmanton)	1812	1812	STRAF/BELKN
Gilmanton	1727	1727	STRAF/BELKN
Gilsum (formerly Boyle)	1752	1763	CHESHIRE
Goffstown (formerly Narragansett No 4)	1733/4	1748	HILLSBOROUGH
Gorham (from Shelburne)	1770	1836	GRAF/COOS
Goshen (formerly part of Sunapee)	1791	1791	CHESH/SULL
Grafton	1761	1761	GRAFTON
Grantham	1761	1761	CHESH/SULL
Greenfield (formerly Lyndefield Addition)	1872	1791	HILLSBOROUGH
Greenland (from Portsmouth)	1721	1704	ROCKINGHAM
Green's Grant unincorporated			COOS
Greenville	1872	1872	HILLSBOROUGH
Groton (formerly Cockermouth)	1761	1792	GRAFTON
Hadley's Purchase unincorporated			COOS
Hale's Location "			CARROLL
Hampstead (formerly Timerlane Parish)	1749	1749	ROCKINGHAM
Hampton	1635	1635	ROCKINGHAM

TOWN (OR INCORPORATED)	GRANTED	NAMED	COUNTY
Hampton Falls 1726 (from Hampton)	1726		ROCKINGHAM
Hancock 1779		1779	HILLSBOROUGH
Hanover 1761		1761	GRAFTON
Harrisville 1870 (formerly Twitcheville)		1870	CHESHIRE
Hart's Location unincorporated			CARROLL
Haverhill 1763 (formerly Lower Coos)		1763	GRAFTON
Hebron 1792 (from Cockermouth)		1792	GRAFTON
Henniker 1735/6 (formerly No 6)		1768	HILLS/MERR
Hill 1753 (formerly New Chester)		1837	GRAF/MERR
Hillsborough 1735/6 (formerly No 7)		1748	HILLSBOROUGH
Hinsdale 1753		1753	CHESHIRE
Holderness 1751		1751	STRAF/GRAF
Hollis 1746		1746	HILLSBOROUGH
Hooksett 1822 (formerly Chester Woods & Rowe's Corner)		1822	HILLS/MERR
Hopkinton 1735/6 (formerly No 5)		1735	HILLS/MERR
Hudson 1746 (formerly Nottingham West)		1741	HILLSBOROUGH
Jackson 1800 (formerly New Madbury & Adams)		1829	GRAF/COOS/ CARR
Jaffrey 1749 (formerly part of Rowley Canada)		1773	CHESHIRE
Jefferson 1765		1796	GRAF/COOS
Keene 1733 (formerly Upper Ashuelot)		1753	CHESHIRE
Kensington 1737		1730	ROCKINGHAM
Kilkenny unincorp'd			COOS
Kinsgston 1694		1694	ROCKINGHAM
Laconia 1855 (from Meredith & Gilford)		1855	BELKNAP
Lancaster 1763		1763	GRAF/COOS
Landaff 1764		1774	GRAFTON
Langdon 1787		1787	CHESH/SULL
Lebanon 1761		1761	GRAFTON
Lee 1766		1766	STRAFFORD
Lempster 1735/6 (formerly No 9 & Dupplin)		1761	CHESH/SULL
Lincoln unincorp'd			GRAFTON
Lisbon 1763 (formerly Concord, Chiswick, & Gunthwaite)		1824	GRAFTON
Litchfield 1729 (formerly Naticook)		1729	HILLSBOROUGH
Littleton 1764 (from Lisbon)		1784	GRAFTON
Livermore unincorp'd			GRAFTON
Londonderry 1722		1722	ROCKINGHAM
Loudon 1773 (from Canterbury)		1773	ROCK/MERR
Lowe and Burbank Grant unincorporated			COOS
Lyman 1761		1761	GRAFTON
Lyme 1761		1761	GRAFTON
Lyndeborough 1735		1735	HILLSBOROUGH
Madbury 1755 (from Durham)		1755	STRAFFORD
Madison 1852 (from Eaton & Albany)		1852	CARROLL
Manchester 1735 (formerly Harrytown, Tyngsboro and Derryfield)		1800s	HILLSBOROUGH
Marlborough 1752 (Monadnock No 5, Oxford, New Marlborough)		1776	CHESHIRE
Marlow 1753 (formerly Addison)		1761	CHESHIRE
Martin's Location unincorporated			COOS
Mason 1749 (formerly No 1)		1768	HILLSBOROUGH
Meredith 1748 (formerly Palmer's Town and New Salem)		1768	STRAF/BELKN
Merrimack 1746 (from Nashua)		1746	HILLSBOROUGH
Middleton 1749		1749	STRAFFORD
Milan 1771 (formerly Paulsborough)		1824	COOS
Milford 1794 (from Monson)		1746	HILLSBOROUGH
Millsfield 1774		1774	GRAF/COOS
Milton 1802 (from Rochester)		1802	STRAFFORD
Monroe 1854 (from Lyman)		1854	GRAFTON
Mont Vernon 1803 (from Amherst)		1803	HILLSBOROUGH
Moultonborough 1763		1763	STRAF/CARR
Nashua 1746 (formerly Dunstable)		1836	HILLSBOROUGH
Nelson 1752 (formerly Monadnock No 6 and Packersfield)		1752	CHESHIRE

TOWN	GRANTED (OR INCORPORATED)	NAMED	COUNTY
New Boston	1735/6	1763	HILLSBOROUGH
New Durham (formerly Cocheco Township)	1749	1762	STRAFFORD
New Hampton (formerly Moultonborough Addition)	1765	1777	STRAF/BELKN
New Ipswich	1735/6	1735	HILLSBOROUGH
New London (formerly Heidelberg & Alexandria Addition)	1753	1779	HILLS/MERR
Newbury (formerly Dantzig, Hereford and Fisherfield)	1753	1837	CHESH/HILLS MERRIMACK
Newcastle (from Portsmouth)	1693	1693	ROCKINGHAM
Newfields (from Newmarket)	1849	1895	ROCKINGHAM
Newington	1764	1714	ROCKINGHAM
Newmarket (from Exeter)	1727	1727	ROCKINGHAM
Newport (formerly Grenville)	1753	1761	CHESH/SULL
Newton (from South Hampton)	1749	1749	ROCKINGHAM
North Hampton (formerly North Hill & North Parish)	1738	1742	ROCKINGHAM
Northfield (from Canterbury)	1780	1780	ROCK/MERR
Northumberland (formerly Stonington)	1761	1771	COOS
Northwood (from Nottingham)	1773	1763	ROCKINGHAM
Nottingham	1722	1722	ROCKINGHAM
Odell	unincorporated		COOS
Orange (formerly Cardigan, Bradford, Middletown & Liscomb)	1769	1790	GRAFTON
Orford	1761	1761	GRAFTON
Ossipee (formerly New Garden)	1785	1785	STRAF/CARR
Pelham	1746	1746	ROCK/HILLS
Pembroke (formerly Lovewell's Town, Suncook & Buckstreet)	1728	1759	ROCK/MERR
Peterborough	1737/8	1738	HILLSBOROUGH
Piermont	1764	1764	GRAFTON
Pinkham's Grant and Pinkham's Notch	unincorporated		COOS
Pittsburg (formerly Indian Stream)	1840	1840	COOS
Pittsfield (from Chichester)	1782	1782	ROCK/MERR
Plainfield	1761	1761	CHESH/SULL
Plaistow (from Haverhill, MA)	1749	1749	ROCKINGHAM
Plymouth (formerly New Plymouth)	1763	1763	GRAFTON
Portsmouth (fomerly Piscataqua & Strawberry Banke)	1631	1653	ROCKINGHAM
Randolph (formerly Durand)	1772	1824	GRAF/COOS
Raymond (from Chester)(formerly Freetown)	1764	1764	ROCKINGHAM
Richmond (formerly Sylvester Canada)	1735	1752	CHESHIRE
Rindge (formerly part of Rowley Canada)	1736/7	1768	CHESHIRE
Rochester	1722	1722	STRAFFORD
Rollinsford (from Somersworth)	1849	1849	STRAFFORD
Roxbury (from Marlborough)	1812	1812	CHESHIRE
Rumney	1761	1761	GRAFTON
Rye (from Portsmouth)	1726	1726	ROCKINGHAM
Salem (formerly North Parish of Methuen, MA)	1750	1741	ROCKINGHAM
Salisbury (formerly Baker's Town, Stevenstown and Gerrishtown)	1736/7	1768	HILLS/MERR
Sanbornton	1748	1748	STRAF/BELKN
Sandown (from Kingston)	1756	1756	ROCKINGHAM
Sandwich	1763	1763	STRAF/CARR
Sargent's Purchase	unincorporated		COOS
Seabrook (from Hampton)	1768	1768	ROCKINGHAM
Second College Grant	unincorporated		COOD
Sharon (from Peterborough)	1791	1738	HILLSBOROUGH
Shelburne	1769	1769	GRAF/COOS
Somersworth (from Dover)	1754	1754	STRAFFORD
South Hampton (from Amesbury, MA & Salisbury, MA)	1742	1742	ROCKINGHAM
Springfield (formerly Protectworth)	1769	1794	CHESH/SULL
Stark (formerly Percy)	1774	1832	GRAF/COOS
Stewartstown	1770	1799	GRAF/COOS

TOWN (OR INCORPORATED)	GRANTED	NAMED	COUNTY
Stoddard	1752	1774	CHESHIRE
(formerly Monadnock No 7 & Limerick)			
Strafford	1820	bef.Rev.	STRAFFORD
Stratford	1762	1773	GRAF/COOS
(formerly Woodbury)			
Stratham	1715/6	1716	ROCKINGHAM
Success	1773	1773	GRAF/COOS
Sugar Hill		1962	GRAFTON
(from Lisbon)			
Sullivan	1787	1787	CHESHIRE
Sunapee	1768	1850	CHESH/SULL
(formerly Saville & Wendell)			
Surry	1769	1769	CHESHIRE
Sutton	1749	1784	HILLS/MERR
(formerly Perrystown)			
Swanzey	1733	1753	CHESHIRE
Tamworth	1766	1766	STRAF/CARR
Temple	1750	1750	HILLSBOROUGH
(formerly part of Peterborough Slip)			
Thompson & Meserve's Purchase	unincorporated		COOS
Thornton	1763	1763	GRAFTON
Tilton	1869	1869	BELKNAP
(from Sanbornton)			
Troy	1815	1815	CHESHIRE
(from Marlborough)			
Tuftonboro	1750	1750	STRAF/CARR
Unity	1753	1764	CHESH/SULL
(formerly Buckingham)			
Wakefield	1749	1774	STRAF/CARR
(formerly Ham's-town, East-town and Watertown)			
Walpole	1736	1761	CHESHIRE
(formerly Bellowstown)			
Warner	1735/6	1774	HILLS/MERR
(formerly New Amesbury, Jennesstown, Waterloo & Ryetown)			
Warren	1763	1764	GRAFTON
Washington	1735/6	1776	CHESH/SULL
(formerly Monadnock No 8, New Concord & Camden)			
Waterville Valley	1829	1976	GRAFTON
(formerly Waterville)			
Weare	1735	1764	HILLSBOROUGH
(formerly Beverly Canada, Halestown, Robiestown & Wearestown)			
Webster	1860	1860	MERRIMACK
(from Boscawen)			
Wentworth	1766	1766	GRAFTON
Wentworth Location	1797	1881	GRAF/COOS

TOWN (OR INCORPORATED)	GRANTED	NAMED	COUNTY
Westmoreland	1735/6	1735	CHESHIRE
(formerly Great Meadow)			
Whitefield	1774	1774	GRAF/COOS
Wilmot	1807	1807	HILLS/MERR
(from Mt. Kearsarge Gore)			
Wilton	1749	1762	HILLSBOROUGH
(formerly No 2)			
Winchester	1733	1773	CHESHIRE
Windham	1741/2	1741	ROCKINGHAM
Windsor	1798	1798	HILLSBOROUGH
(formerly Campbell's Gore)			
Wolfeborough	1759	1759	STRAF/CARR
Woodstock	1763	1840	GRAFTON
(formerly Peeling & Fairfield)			

CENSUS RECORDS - FEDERAL

The New Hampshire State Library has original U. S. Census schedules for 1850 through 1880; also 1840 for Rockingham, Merrimack, Strafford counties. Microfilm copies of 1800 through 1880; printed copies of 1790 and 1800. Printed indexes to 1810 and 1820. The New Hampshire Historical Society has a photostat of the 1800 census. U.S. Census records for New Hampshire (1800 - 1910) are available from the NATIONAL ARCHIVES - BOSTON BRANCH at 380 Trapelo Road in Waltham, Mass. (see entry under Massachusetts - Census Records - Federal)

****

CENSUS RECORDS - STATE

There are no state census records for New Hampshire.

****

PROBATE AND LAND RECORDS

BELKNAP COUNTY (Established 1840 from Strafford and Merrimack Counties)
64 Court Street
Laconia, NH 03246

Register of Probate   603-524-0903
  Mon-Fri 8-4:30 (July-Aug 8-4)
  Directions: Courthouse at intersection
  of Rte 3 & 106 in downtown Laconia.

Probate Records: 1841-present
Staff-operated photocopying:
.50/page.
Wills $2 1st page. .50 ea. addl.

Register of Deeds   603-524-8618
  Mon-Fri 8:30-4

Deeds: 1840-present. Volumes on open shelves & can be consulted. Register also has typed copies of Strafford Cty deeds pertaining to Belknap Cty land, 1771-1840. Deeds: $1 1st page. $.25 each additional page.

CARROLL COUNTY (Established 1840 from Strafford County)
Ossipee, NH 03864
  Directions: NH Routes 16 or 28 to
  Ossipee. West on NH Rte 171 one mile.
Register of Probate   603-539-4123
  Mon-Fri 9-5

Register of Deeds   603-539-4872
  Mon-Fri 9-5

Probate Records: 1840-present. Index on cards. Records retrieved by staff. Staff-operated photocopying. Min. Chrg $1. Wills: $2 1st page. 50 c. addl. Deeds: 1841-present. Indexes & vols. on open shelves. Copies $1/page. Plans $5/page.

CHESHIRE COUNTY (Established 1769)
   12 Court Street
   Keene, NH 03431
      Directions: Central Sq. Corner
      of Court & Winter Sts.

Probate Records: 1771-present.
Staff-operated copying $2 1st
page of will; .50 ea. addl. Other
records .50/image.

   Register of Probate   603-352-0050 Ext 72
      Mon-Fri 8:30-12:30; 1:30-5   (Summer 8-12:30; 1:30-4:30)
   Register of Deeds   603-352 0050 Ext 50
      Mon-Fri 9-5 (Summer 4:30)

Deeds: 1771-present. Staff-copies
$1/page. Pre-paid by mail.
50 c. extra for certification.

COOS COUNTY (Established 1803 from Grafton County)
   148 Main Street
   Lancaster, NH 03584
      Directions: U.S.Rte 3, 200 yds
      north of center of town.
   Register of Probate   603-788-2001
      Mon-Fri 9-12, 1-4

Probate records: 1887-present.
On open shelves. (Prior records
destroyed by fire.) Staff copies.
Varying costs.

   Register of Deeds   603-788-2392
      Mon-Fri 8-12, 1-4

Deeds: 1803-present. (Some back
to 1700.) 7 vols of Grafton Co.
deeds for Coos County land.
Copies $1   (By mail: $2)

GRAFTON COUNTY (Established 1769)
   Woodsville, NH 03774
      Directions: on State Rte 10.
   Register of Probate   603-787-6931
      Mon-Fri 8-4

Probate records: 1773-present.
Card index. Pre-1800 records must
be viewed on microfilm. Staff
copies up to $2.

   Register of Deeds   603-787-6921
      Mon-Fri 8:30-4

Deeds: 1773-present. 1st 16 vols
must be viewed on microfilm.
Copies up to $1.50/page.

HILLSBOROUGH COUNTY (Established 1769)
   19 Temple Street
   Nashua, NH 03061
      Directions: Everett Tpk to Rte 111
      to Nashua. Left on Rte 3. 3rd right
      onto Temple.

Probate records: 1771-present.

   Register of Probate   603-882-1231
      Mon-Fri 8:30-4:45

Deeds: 1771-present. Deed books
1919 plus indexes in basement
vault. Later vols. on 1st floor.
Vols. 1-present on microfilm. But
originals may be consulted. Coin
copier available. Staff-copying
.50/page plus postage if mailed.

   Register of Deeds   603-882-6933
      Mon-Fri 8-4

MERRIMACK COUNTY (Established 1823 from Rockingham & Hillsborough Counties)

163 North Main Street
Concord, NH 03301
  Directions: Rte 93 to Rte 4/202
(exit 14) West to lights. Turn right
on N. Main St. Courthouse on left.
Parking in rear.
Register of Probate   603-224-9589
  Mon-Fri 8:30-5 (4:30 in summer)

Register of Deeds   603-228-0101
  P. O. Box 248
  Mon-Fri 8-4:30

Probate records: 1823-present. Card index. Recs on microfilm but originals may be consulted. Copies $1/page. (Inventory & accounts, $5.) One micro-printer. Several Micro-readers. Service by mail. Rates same as above.

Deeds: 1823-present. 1st 634 vols (to 1940) on cards which must be retrieved by clerk. Staff copies $2 covers 2 pgs of one deed. .25 thereafter. Plans: $3. 6 micro-readers; 2 printers. Service by mail. Rates same as above.

ROCKINGHAM COUNTY (Established 1769)

Administration and Justice Building
Exeter, NH 03833
  Directions: Jct of State Rts 101-C
& 88. Free parking.

Register of Probate   603-772-9347
  Mon-Fri 8-4:30
  Summer 7:30-4

Register of Deeds   603-772-4712
  Mon-Fri 8-4:30
  Summer 7:30-4

Probate records: 1770-present. Card index. Self-service. Records microfilmed, but originals may be consulted. Must sign book for each rec. used. Vols 31-39 of State Papers; town histories for Rock. Cty; Index to Hillsborough County Probate. Staff copies .50/page.

Deeds: 1630-present. Pre-1771 records called "NH Province Deeds" Deeds 1-296 on cards. Staff copies .75/pg. $2/pg for indexes. Service by mail.

STRAFFORD COUNTY (Established 1769)

Justice and Administration Building
County Farm Road
Dover, NH 03820
  Directions: Spaulding Tpk to Exit 9;
follow signs to Justice & Admin. Bldg.

Register of Probate   603-742-2550
  Mon-Fri 8-4:30

Register of Deeds   603-742-1741
  Mon-Fri 8:30-4:30

Probate Records: 1769-present. Self-service. Post 1900 index on cards. Staff copying .50/image

Deeds: 1770-present. Vols. 1-23 & 38 on cards. Vols 24-present original vols. Staff copying $1/pg. 1 microfilm reader. One microfilm printer.

SULLIVAN COUNTY (Established 1827 from Cheshire County)

24 Main Street
Newport, NH 03773
Mailing Address: P.O. Box 417
   Directions: State Rte 10 to Newport
Bldg on East Side of Main St.

Register of Probate   603-863-3150
   Mon-Fri 8:30-5

Register of Deeds   603-863-2110
   Mon-Fri 8:30-4:30

Probate Records: 1827-present.
Early indexes by 1st letter of
surname only. All in vault.
Staff access only. Staff copying
.50/page.

Deeds: 1827-present. Some early
vols. partially burned. Staff
copying. $1/1st pg. .50 addl.
Plus postage if by mail.

****

CEMETERY RECORDS

The NEW HAMPSHIRE HISTORICAL SOCIETY (see entry under New Hampshire-Libraries) has a large collection of inscriptions copied from gravestones in New Hampshire cemeteries. For a list of their holdings, see the Winter 1975 and Spring 1980 issues of Historical New Hampshire.

The NEW HAMPSHIRE OLD GRAVEYARD ASSOCIATION (See entry under New Hampshire Societies)

****

CHURCH RECORDS

Original records are usually found at the church. When a church was discontinued, the records were sometimes deposited with the state organization. Many churches have deposited their early records in the NEW HAMPSHIRE HISTORICAL SOCIETY. Other libraries may have a few records. Quaker Records for all New England are at the Rhode Island Historical Society Library.

****

MILITARY RECORDS

THE NEW HAMPSHIRE ARCHIVES AND RECORD CENTER (see address below) has the records of the French and Indian Wars with a name index. These records were printed in the Adjutant General's Report Vol. ii, 1866, and the N.H. Provincial and State Papers, Vols. 5, 6, 14, 16. The ARCHIVES AND RECORDS CENTER also has Revolutionary War Records. These were published in N.H. Provincial and State Papers, Vols. 14-17 and 30. Also Civil War Records arranged alphabetically by surname, published by the Adjutant General in Revised Register of Soldiers and Sailors of New Hampshire in the War of the Rebellion, 1895.

Pension records for soldiers and sailors who fought in the Revolutionary War are in the National Archives in Washington D.C. and can be requested by using proper forms. The NEW HAMPSHIRE HISTORICAL SOCIETY has an alphabetical typed transcript consisting of 71 volumes for the New Hampshire soldiers who received pensions.

NEW HAMPSHIRE

LIBRARIES

CONCORD - <u>NEW HAMPSHIRE DIVISION OF RECORDS MANAGEMENT AND ARCHIVES</u>

   71 South Fruit Street   From south: Rte 93 to Exit 12 (Rte 3A).
   Concord, NH 03301   North 2 blocks to Broadway. North 1 mile
   603-271-2236   to flashing light. (Rt 13). Left onto
   Mon-Fri 8-4:30   Clinton. 2nd right onto South Fruit.
                             From north, Rte 93 to Rte 202 to Pleasant
                             St. to South Fruit.

No fees. Photocopying machine .20/page. 2 microfilm readers. 1 reader/printer. 75 cents/page. Copies by mail depending on physical condition and/or confidentiality of document. Payment must be made in cash, check or money order payable to State of New Hampshire. No interlibrary loan. <u>Holdings</u>: Provincial and State Records, Court Records (including Probate), records relating to towns, Military and Revolutionary Records. For a further description of holdings, see Frank C. Mevers and Harriet S. Lacy, "Early Historical Records (c1620-c1817) at the New Hampshire State Archives," in <u>Historical New Hampshire</u>, vol 31 (1976) pp 108-118, and <u>Guide to Early Documents at the N.H. Records Management and Archives Center</u> (1981).

CONCORD - <u>NEW HAMPSHIRE HISTORICAL SOCIETY LIBRARY</u>

   30 Park Street   Rte 93 to Exit 14 (Bridge Street).
   Concord, NH 03301   West 2 blocks. Left on North State
   603-225-3381   St. 1st right on Park St.
   Mon, Tues, Thurs, Fri 9-4:30
   Wed 9-8 p.m.

No fees. Some open stacks. Staff-operated photocopying service .20/page non-members. 2 microfilm readers. 1 reader/printer. Copies by mail $3 minimum charge. No extensive searches. No interlibrary loan. <u>Holdings</u>: Printed and manuscript genealogies, town and local histories, newspapers, cemetery inscriptions, church records. Card index of New Hampshire notables. Province probate records, 1655-1771 (microfilm); Province deeds, 1630-1770 (microfilm). This is the finest library for the study of New Hampshire genealogy, local history and biography.

CONCORD - <u>NEW HAMPSHIRE STATE LIBRARY</u>

   20 Park Street   Rte 93 to Exit 14 (Bridge St.) Rte. 202
   Concord, NH 03301   West 1 block. Left on No. Main St.
   603-271-2144 (Ref. Desk)   Right on Park St. On-street metered
   Mon-Fri 8:30-4:30   parking.

No fees: Genealogies are in closed stack area. Photocopying .10/page. 2 microfilm readers. 2 printers. .25/frame. Library does not undertake genealogical research. Materials do not circulate. <u>Holdings</u>: Copies of Town Records of most New Hampshire towns prior to 1835 (L.D.S. microfilm copies). Master card index to all the names appearing in the above (called the "Sargent Index") Manuscript of U.S. Censuses for New Hampshire 1850-1880; manuscript of 1840 Census for Rockingham, Strafford, Merrimack Counties. Microfilm of U.S. Census for New Hampshire 1800-1830. Many 20th century New Hampshire newspapers on microfilm.

DOVER - <u>DOVER</u> <u>PUBLIC</u> <u>LIBRARY</u>

    73 Locust Street   From Spaulding Turnpike, take Exit 8
    Dover, NH 03820   (Silver St. - Rte 9) to downtown Dover.
    603-742-3513   Library behind City Hall, corner of
    Mon-Thurs 9-8:30   Locust & Hale. Parking behind library.
    Fri 9-5:30

No fees, but patron must "sign in" at reference desk to use locked genealogy and local history room. Photocopying .10/page. 1 microfilm reader. Staff cannot undertake research. Will answer brief questions or check catalog. Materials do not circulate. <u>Holdings</u>: One of the best and largest collections of printed books and periodicals on New Hampshire genealogy and local history in the state. Many rare books and pamphlets relating to Dover area history. Dover newspapers on microfilm back to 1823 (in Reference Room).

DURHAM - <u>DIMOND</u> <u>LIBRARY,</u> <u>UNIVERSITY</u> <u>OF</u> <u>NEW</u> <u>HAMPSHIRE</u>

    Dover, NH 03824   Rte 4 to Durham. Follow signs to UNH
    603-862-1540   campus (on Main St., west of town center)
    Mon-Fri 9-12, 1-4:30   Ample parking. Special collections
                              department, 3rd floor.

No fees. Photocopying service. Microfilm readers. No research done by staff. Materials do not circulate. <u>Holdings</u>: Large collection of New Hampshire genealogy and local history. An inventory of the Lamson Collection was published in <u>Piscataqua</u> <u>Pioneers</u> <u>List</u> <u>of</u> <u>New</u> <u>Members,</u> <u>1978</u>.

EXETER - <u>EXETER</u> <u>PUBLIC</u> <u>LIBRARY</u>

    86 Front Street   On Front St. (Rte 111) at corner of
    Exeter, NH 03833   Spring St. 2 blocks west of center of
    603-772-3101   town, next to Phillips Exeter Academy.
    Mon-Fri 10-8, Sat 10-5 On-street parking.

No fees. Ask at reference desk to use locked Genealogy and Local History Room. Photocopying .10/page. 1 microfilm reader. 1 reader/printer, .10/copy. Staff cannot undertake research. Will answer brief questions and check catalog. Materials do not circulate. <u>Holdings</u>: Small collection of local history and genealogy relating to Eastern New Hampshire. Exeter <u>Newsletter</u> (newspaper) on microfilm, 1831-present.

HANOVER - <u>BAKER</u> <u>LIBRARY</u> - <u>DARTMOUTH</u> <u>COLLEGE</u>

    Hanover, NH 03755   State Rte 10 to Hanover. Library is on
    603-646-2560   North St. (Rte 10) just north of
    Mon-Fri 8-4:30   downtown Hanover. Street parking.

No fees. Two photocopying machines, .05/copy. Microfilm reader. Except for the ref. area, stacks are closed and books must be retrieved by staff. Staff cannot answer general genealogical queries by mail unless they relate to Hanover/Dartmouth persons. Jones Microtext Room is open and should be consulted. Materials do not circulate.

KEENE - <u>KEENE PUBLIC LIBRARY</u>
    79 West Street
    Keene, NH 03431
    603-352-0157

From downtown Keene, turn onto West St.
which is on west side of square.
Library is on the right.

No fees. Photocopying .10/page. Microfilm reader. Genealogies kept in the "Wright Room." No interlibrary loan.

MANCHESTER - <u>AMERICAN CANADIAN GENEALOGICAL SOCIETY LIBRARY</u>
    St. Anthony's Church   Friday: 9-9:30
    172 Belmont Street   (other times by appointment)
    So. Manchester, NH 03103

Perhaps the best library in New England for tracing French-Canadian ancestry. (See also entry under New Hampshire - Societies)

NASHUA - <u>NASHUA, NH BRANCH GENEALOGICAL LIBRARY</u>
    Church of Jesus Christ of Latter-Day Saints
    110 Concord Street
    Nashua, NH 03060
    603-880-7371
    Wed, Thurs 10-2; 7-10
    Sat 9-5

From the south: Rte 3 (Everett Tpk) take Exit 7 E at Amherst St. At top of ramp go straight thru traffic light at end of road. Turn right on Concord St. Church is on right 1/2 mile.
From north: Rte 3 Exit 7 E. Cross bridge (Rt 3), turn left at traffic light onto Henry Burque Hwy. (see above directions)

Fees: Rolls of microfilm $2.35 ea. for a 2-wk loan of film from Salt Lake City. $3.35 for 6 months. 5 microfilm readers; 6 microfiche readers + reader/printer (.25/copy). Service by mail if patron knows exact film number and sends check. Staff is volunteer. No Interlibrary loans. <u>Holdings</u>: Microfilmed Card Catalog (MCC), International Genealogical Index (IGI), Genealogical Library Catalog (GLC), Accelerated Indexing Systems (AIS), and Family Registry; 283 Family Group Record Archive (FGRA) films on Indefinite Loan, and 219 other Indefinite Loan films, with an emphasis on N.E. and Maritime Provinces; Strafford, NH deeds on microfilm, Vols. 1-207 (1771-1851) plus grantor-grantee indexes. Complete set of Research Papers by the Genealogical Dept. in Salt Lake on countries of major genealogical interest; two World Conference on Records held in Salt Lake on film and book. Small collection of "how-to" books and other miscellaneous books.

****

SOCIETIES

THE AMERICAN-CANADIAN GENEALOGICAL SOCIETY

P.O. Box 668
Manchester, NH 03103
603-622-2883

Library located in the basement of
L'Association Canado-Americaine on
52 Concord St., Manchester, NH

Founded: September 1973 "to encourage the gathering of all types of genealogical records, to acquire genealogical records for the library, to encourage individual members to research their family lineage and to contribute a copy to the library, to serve as a resource center for American-Canadian Genealogy."

Dues: $10/yr individual; $5/yr each additional family member; $150 Life Member. Publication: "The Genealogist" publ. quarterly (with membership). Meetings: First weekend in May and first weekend in October held in Manchester, NH.

THE NEW HAMPSHIRE HISTORICAL SOCIETY

30 Park Street
Concord, NH 03301
603-225-3381

Directions: Rte 93 to exit 14 (Bridge St) West on Bridge St. 2 blocks. Left on North State St. First right onto Park Street.

Founded: 1823 "to collect material relating to New Hampshire history and decorative arts." Dues: $15 and up per year. Meetings: Annual meeting 1st Saturday in April.

Publication: "Historical New Hampshire" (quarterly) (with membership). An historical rather than genealogical publication. Queries not accepted. Articles submitted should be the result of original research and pertain to some aspect of New Hampshire's past. First issue: November 1944.

THE NEW HAMPSHIRE SOCIETY OF GENEALOGISTS

P.O. Box 633
Exeter, NH 03833

Founded: April 1978 "to bring together genealogists, historians, librarians and all others interested in the history of mankind. To preserve records, to insure public access of records and to function in any capacity needed to assist those desiring to trace their lineage."

Dues: $4 per year. Newsletter published quarterly. A Family Register is maintained by the Society covering individuals and families known to have resided in the Province or State prior to 1901. Write for complete information. Meetings: Twice annually, fall and spring, in the Concord area. Local chapters have meetings throughout the year. (Two of the county chapters, Rockingham and Strafford, have newsletters also.)

NEW HAMPSHIRE

THE NEW HAMPSHIRE OLD GRAVEYARD ASSOCIATION (NHOGA)
Carleton R. Vance, Corresponding Secretary
445 Greeley Street
Manchester, NH 03102

Founded: 1975 "to study New Hampshire gravestones and cemeteries for their artistic, historic, cultural and genealogical value. To help preserve New Hampshire's old cemeteries."

Dues: $3 per year individual; $5 per year for organizations. Meetings: three per year. Annual meetings in the spring at various locations. Publication: Newsletter - NHOGA Rubbings free with membership. Book: Graveyard Restoration Hand Book $1.50.

THE PISCATAQUA PIONEERS
Mr. Edward G. Wood, Registrar   Mrs. William Haubrich, Curator
One Tobey Street   9 Lindy Avenue
Hampton, NH 03842   Claremont, NH 03743

Founded: 15 June 1905 "to secure and preserve the records of the Pioneers of the Piscataqua Valley between Maine and New Hampshire and of their descendants. To promote fellowship among members."

Dues: $5 per year. $50 life membership. $5 initial fee. Meetings: Annual meeting last Saturday in July at Portsmouth, NH - various locations. The Curator is in charge of application papers and keeping up-to-date record of reference material held in the Lamson Collection at the Dimond Library at UNH in Durham.

****

BOOKS AND ARTICLES

Belknap, Jeremy. The History of New Hampshire, 3 volumes. Philadelphia, 1784; Boston, 1791, 1792.

Copeley, William, "Family Names in New Hampshire Town Histories, 1947-1980," Historical New Hampshire. Winter, 1980.

Dearborn, David C. "New Hampshire Genealogy: A Perspective," in The New England Historical and Genealogical Register, 130 (1976) : 244-58.

Hanrahan, E. J., ed., Hammond's Checklist of New Hampshire History, Somersworth, NH, 1971.

Hunt, Elmer M. "Family Names in New Hampshire Town Histories," in Historical New Hampshire, December 1946.

Hunt, Elmer M. New Hampshire Town Names; and Whence They Came. Peterborough, 1970.

The New Hampshire Genealogical Record. 7 volumes, Dover, NH, 1903-1910. (New Hampshire Historical Society has typescript master index.)

New Hampshire Provincial and State Papers, 40 volumes, Concord and Manchester, NH, 1867-1943. For a good discussion of their contents, see R. Stuart Wallace, "The State Papers: A Descriptive Guide," in Historical New Hampshire, 31: 119-28.

Noyes, Sybil; Libby, Charles T.; Davis, Walter G., Genealogical Dictionary of Maine and New Hampshire, Portland, 1828-39: reprint ed. Baltimore, MD: Genealogical Publishing Company, 1972-1976.

Pope, Charles H., The Pioneers of Maine and New Hampshire, Boston, 1908; reprint ed. Baltimore, Genealogical Publishing Co., 1973.

Stearns, Ezra S., Genealogical and Family History of the State of New Hampshire, 4 volumes, Chicago, 1908.

Towle, Laird C., and Brown, Ann N., New Hampshire Genealogical Research Guide, Bowie, MD: Heritage Books, 1983.

****

RHODE ISLAND

0 1 2 3 4 5 miles

SCALE

MASS.

WOONSOCKET

NORTH

SMITHFIELD

CUMBERLAND

BURRILLVILLE

LINCOLN

GLOCESTER

SMITHFIELD

CENTRAL
FALLS

PAWTUCKET

NORTH
PROVIDENCE

JOHNSTON

PROVIDENCE

FOSTER

SCITUATE

EAST
PROVIDENCE

N

CRANSTON

BARRINGTON

CONN.

WARREN

WEST

WARWICK

BRISTOL

COVENTRY

WARWICK

EAST
GREENWICH

WEST GREENWICH

PORTSMOUTH

TIVERTON

EXETER

NORTH
KINGSTOWN

JAMESTOWN

MIDDLE-
TOWN

LITTLE

COMPTON

RICHMOND

HOPKINTON

SOUTH KINGSTOWN

NEWPORT

CHARLESTOWN

NARRAGANSETT

WESTERLY

BLOCK
ISLAND

NEW
SHOREHAM

RHODE ISLAND

Genealogical research in Rhode Island can be an interesting and enjoyable experience. There is a wealth of primary source material available for study - much of it well-indexed and in reasonably good condition. Because Rhode Island is small geographically, it is possible to travel easily from one end of the state to the other to examine materials first-hand. Most libraries and other institutions welcome researchers and willingly provide assistance. Mail requests are usually answered, and referrals are given to other possible sources of information. The Rhode Island Historical Society Library in Providence is highly recommended as the place for a beginning researcher to visit first, since their collection is the most extensive in the state.

****

VITAL RECORDS - 1636 to 1850

See Vital Record of Rhode Island, 1636-1850, by James N. Arnold. (Providence, The Narragansett Historical Publishing Company) 1911. 21 volumes. Available at many major libraries. See also: Beaman, Rhode Island Genealogical Register, p. 128)

VITAL RECORDS - 1850 to 1853

Records for these three years are only available at the town or city clerk's office.

VITAL RECORDS - 1853 to present

RHODE ISLAND DEPARTMENT OF HEALTH
DIVISION OF VITAL STATISTICS
    Cannon Building - Room 101
    75 Davis Street
    Providence, Rhode Island 02908
    401-277-2811
    Mon-Fri 8:30-4:30
    Directions: Near RI State House

Holdings: Birth, marriage, death records, 1853 to present. Service by mail: $5 per search of up to two years includes copy of document. Checks or money orders to "General Treasurer - State of Rhode Island."

(Note: See also: Beaman, Rhode Island Genealogical Register, p. 128.)

****

CENSUS RECORDS - FEDERAL

THE ARCHIVES OF THE STATE OF RHODE ISLAND (See entry under RHODE ISLAND - LIBRARIES - PROVIDENCE)

NATIONAL ARCHIVES - BOSTON BRANCH (See entry under MASSACHUSETTS - CENSUS RECORDS - FEDERAL)

RHODE ISLAND HISTORICAL SOCIETY LIBRARY (See entry under RHODE ISLAND - LIBRARIES - PROVIDENCE)

CENSUS RECORDS - STATE

THE ARCHIVES OF THE STATE OF RHODE ISLAND (See entry under RHODE ISLAND - LIBRARIES - PROVIDENCE)

RHODE ISLAND RECORDS CENTER
    83 Park Street
    Providence, RI 02903
    401-277-2283
    Mon-Fri 8:30-4:30
    Directions: One block west of
    State House. In basement of
    Veterans Memorial Auditorium.

Holdings: Rhode Island State Census for 1905, 1915, 1925, 1935. The 1905 census is filed alphabetically by family name and town. Others filed by census district. No copying facilities. Limited service by mail.

(Note: Rhode Island state census records 1774-1782 are in print.)

****

PROBATE AND LAND RECORDS

Probate and Land Records (as well as Vital Records) are located in each individual city and town hall. Sometimes earlier records are held by a town different from the town holding the current records.

TOWN	FOUNDED	RECORDS	TOWN/CITY HALL
BARRINGTON	1717 From Mass. as part of the new town of Warren in 1747; Re-established as Barrington in 1770	bef. 1747 1747-1770	Taunton, MA 514 Main St. Warren RI
		1770-	283 County Road Barrington, RI
BRISTOL	1681 From Mass. in 1747; Called Mt. Hope in 1679	bef. 1747 1747-	Taunton, MA Town Hall, Bristol, RI
BURRILVILLE	1806 From Glocester	bef. 1806 1806-	Glocester, RI 02814 70 Main Street Harrisville, RI 02830
CENTRAL FALLS	1895 From Lincoln	1895-	580 Broad Street Central Falls, RI 02863
CHARLESTOWN	1738 From Westerly	bef. 1738 1738-	Westerly, RI P.O. Box 372 Charlestown, RI
COVENTRY	1741 From Warwick	(some) 1741-	75 Main Street Coventry, RI

RHODE ISLAND

TOWN	FOUNDED		RECORDS	TOWN/CITY HALL
CRANSTON	1754 From Providence		1754-	City Hall Cranston, RI 02910
CUMBERLAND	1747 from Mass. Formerly called Attleboro Gore	Land 1692- Probate 1896-		45 Broad Street Cumberland, RI
E. GREENWICH	1677 Called Dedford 1686-1689	Land 1679- Probate 1715-		P.O. Box 111, E. Greenwich 02818
E. PROVIDENCE	1862 From Mass.; Originally Rehoboth, then Seekonk		1816-1862 1862-	Taunton, MA 145 Taunton Avenue E. Providence, RI
EXETER	1743 From North Kingstown		1742-	Victory Highway Exeter, RI 02822
FOSTER	1781 From Scituate		1781-	South Killingly Road Foster RI 02825
GLOCESTER	1731 From Providence		1731-	Main Street Chepachet, RI 02814
HOPKINTON	1757 From Westerly		1757-	Town House Road Hopkinton, RI 02833
JAMESTOWN	1678 Indian name Conanicut		1678-	71 Narragansett Ave. Jamestown, RI
JOHNSTON	1759 From Providence	Probate 1759-1898 1898- Land 1759-		Providence, RI 02903 1385 Hartford Avenue Johnston, RI 1385 Hartford Avenue Johnston, RI
LINCOLN	1871 From Smithfield		1871-1895 1895-	Central Falls, RI 02863 Lonsdale, RI
LITTLE COMPTON	1682 From Mass. in 1747		bef. 1747 1747-	Taunton, MA Little Compton 02887
MIDDLETOWN	1743 From Newport		1742-	350 East Main Road Middletown, RI 02840
NARRAGANSETT	1901 From South Kingstown		1888-	25 Fifth Avenue Narragansett 02882

TOWN	FOUNDED	RECORDS	TOWN/CITY/HALL
NEWPORT	1639 Original Town	1639-1783	Newport Historical Society
		1783-	City Clerk Newport, RI 02840
		1779-1841	Microfilm of wills
	and inventories at Rhode Island Historical Society		
	Docket Books 9/1884-9/1902 at Newport Historical Society		
NEW SHOREHAM	1661 Admitted to Colony in 1664 as Block Island; Incorporated and name changed in 1672	1674-	Block Island RI 02807
N. KINGSTOWN	1641 Incorporated as Kingstown in 1674; called Rochester 1686-1689; called North Kingstown after 1723	1674-	Wickford, RI 02852
N. PROVIDENCE	1765 From Providence	1765-1874	City Hall Pawtucket, RI 02860
		1874-	Centredale, RI
N. SMITHFIELD	1871 From Smithfield; called Slater for 16 days in 1871	1871-	Slatersville, RI 02876
PAWTUCKET	1828 Part from Mass. in 1862; Part from N. Providence 1874	1828-1862	Taunton, MA
		1862-	City Hall, Pawtucket, RI 02860
PORTSMOUTH	1638 Original Town; called Pocasset until 1639	1636-	2200 East Main Road Portsmouth, RI
PROVIDENCE	1636 Original Town	1636-	25 Dorrance Street Providence, RI 02903
RICHMOND	1747 From Charlestown	bef. 1747	Westerly, RI
		1747-	Wyoming, RI
SCITUATE	1731 From Providence	1731-	Main Street N. Scituate, RI 02857
SMITHFIELD	1731 From Providence	1731-1870	City Clerk's Office Central Falls, RI 02863
		1871-	Georgiaville, RI
S. KINGSTOWN	1723 From Kingstown when divided into North and South	1674-1723	Wickford, RI
		1723-	66 High Street Wakefield, RI 02879
TIVERTON	1694 From Mass. in 1747	bef. 1747	Taunton, MA
		1747-	Tiverton, RI

TOWN	FOUNDED	RECORDS	TOWN/CITY/HALL
WARREN	1747 From Mass. towns of Barrington, Swansea &	bef. 1747 1747-	Taunton, MA Warren, RI
WARWICK	Original town Called Shawmet until 1648	1647	Apponaug, RI 02886
WESTERLY	1669 Called Haversham 1686-1689 and inventories at Rhode Island	1669- 1669-1877	Westerly, RI 02891 Microfilm of wills Historical Society
W. GREENWICH	1741 From East Greenwich	1741-	Victory Hwy, RR 2 West Greenwich, RI
W. WARWICK	1913 From Warwick	1913-	West Warwick, RI
WOONSOCKET	1867 Part from Cumberland in 1867; part from Smithfield in 1871	1867-	Woonsocket, RI

****

CEMETERY RECORDS

Edwin W. Connelly's List of Historical Cemeteries in Rhode Island (1970) lists, by city or town, each historical numbered cemetery and any pertinent information known about the burial ground. Usually included are name of burial ground (if any), owner, exact location, number of graves, condition, and number of veterans buried there.

David W. Dumas'S Rhode Island Grave Records: A Bibiliography is an 8-page pamphlet compiled in 1977, listing grave records available locally to the public. He discusses general sources and then lists, by city or town, specific items to consult before beginning graveyard research.

Copies of the above guides are at the Rhode Island Historical Society Library and a few other libraries in the state.

****

CHURCH AND SYNAGOGUE RECORDS

Most churches and synagogues maintain their own records and each parish, church or synagogue should be consulted individually. One very dated source is the Guide to Church Vital Statistics Records in the State of Rhode Island: A Supplement to the Guide to Public Vital Statistics, compiled and published in 1942 by the Works Progress Administration. The volume is owned by the Rhode Island Historical Society Library and may be available in other libraries. More recent information is available at Rhode Island Archives.

Quaker (Friends) Records for all of New England are at the Rhode Island Historical Society Library. (See entry under RHODE ISLAND - LIBRARIES - PROVIDENCE.)

****

MILITARY RECORDS

THE ARCHIVES OF THE STATE OF RHODE ISLAND (See entry under RHODE ISLAND - LIBRARIES - PROVIDENCE)

Note: Two titles available at large libraries in Rhode Island are: Rhode Island. Adjutant General's Office Annual Report of the Adjutant General for 1865. (2 vols. Providence, Freeman, 1893-1895. Official Register of Men who Served in the U.S. Army and Navy, 1861-1865) and Smith, Joseph Jencks. Civil and Military List of Rhode Island 1747-1800. Supplement 1800-1850. Providence, Preston & Rounds, 1901.

****

LIBRARIES

Most towns in Rhode Island have public libraries. Their holdings vary greatly. For a list of all libraries, consult the American Library Directory in most large libraries, to see what is available and the hours of service.

EAST GREENWICH - EAST GREENWICH FREE LIBRARY
82 Peirce Street   One block above and parallel to Main St.
East Greenwich, RI 02818
401-884-9511
Mon-Fri 10-5, 7-9; Sat 10-5

Photocopy machine. .10/copy. 1 microfilm reader, 1 microfiche reader, 1 microfilm reader/printer. Materials do not circulate. No Interlibrary Loan. Holdings: Rhode Island genealogy, East Greenwich families, a few manuscripts. Approximately 50 volumes in the collection.

NEWPORT - NEWPORT HISTORICAL SOCIETY LIBRARY
82 Touro Street   Next door to Touro Synagogue
Newport, RI 02840
401-846-0813
Tues-Fri 9:30-4:15, Sat 9:30-12
Mid-July - mid-Sept, open all day Sat.

Photocopy machine .25/copy. 1 microfilm reader; 1 reader/printer. .25/copy. Service by mail. $10 research fee per letter. Materials do not circulate. Interlibrary Loan by photocopy/microcopy. Holdings: Pre-Revolutionary Newport Town Records; church records; Rhode Island and Newport familiy genealogies. Correspondence file. Manuscript material including logs, diaries, etc. Newport County History.

NEWPORT - <u>NEWPORT PUBLIC LIBRARY</u>
P.O. Box 8
Spring Street/Aquidneck Park
Newport, RI 02840
Mon. 12:30-9;
Tues-Thurs 9:30-9
Fri, Sat 9:30-6

Directions: Follow Rte 24 to Rte 114. Rte 114 turns into West Main Rd, which turns into Broadway. Go through Washington Square to Thames St. Follow Thames St. past Post Office. Turn left onto Brewer St. which leads directly into library parking lot.

Open to the public. Photocopying machine $.10 per copy. <u>Holdings</u>: Mainly genealogical books on Newport (with some on RI in general). Census records and some land and probate records on microfilm.

PROVIDENCE - <u>BROWN UNIVERSITY, JOHN HAY LIBRARY</u>
Prospect Street
Providence, RI 02912
401-863-2146
Mon-Fri 9-4:30

Metered on-street parking.

No research fee. Must present some form of identification. Staff-operated photocopy machine. $.10/copy. 1 microfilm reader; 1 reader/printer. $.10/copy. Service by mail limited. Materials do not circulate. No Interlibrary Loan. <u>Holdings</u>: Revolutionary War pension applications and supporting documents. Each volume has a separate index. Early Rhode Island records; published family genealogies, manuscript information on Brown University graduates (in archives).

PROVIDENCE - <u>KNIGHT MEMORIAL LIBRARY</u>
275 Elmwood Avenue
Providence, RI 02907
401-521-8769
Mon, Wed, Thur, Fri 9-5
Tues 12-8; Sat 9-5

Elmwood Ave. Exit off Rte 95. Next to United Camera. Free parking.

Photocopy machine $.10/copy. Mail answered. $.25/sheet for copies via mail. Materials do not circulate. No Interlibrary Loan. <u>Holdings</u>: Arnold notes - family and genealogical materials; Bible histories with family notes, tombstone records (indexed). The Arnold Collection was donated to the library in the 1920s. At that time it was the best genealogical collection in Rhode Island. Scrapbook of newspaper clippings - indexed. Revolutionary War notes.

PROVIDENCE - <u>PROVIDENCE ATHENAEUM</u>
251 Benefit Street
Providence, RI 02903
401-421-6970
Mon-Fri 8:30-5:30, Sat 9:30-5:30

Corner of College and Benefit Streets. Parking limited.

Only members can take out books. Anyone can use the library for special projects. Staff-operated photocopy machine $.10/copy. Interlibrary Loan honored. <u>Holdings</u>: General collection of Rhode Island family genealogies. Not unique.

RHODE ISLAND

PROVIDENCE - PROVIDENCE PUBLIC LIBRARY
    150 Empire Street   Near Providence Civic Center, next
    Providence, RI 02903   to Police Station. Parking very poor.
    401-521-7722
    Central Library: Mon-Thurs 9:30-9; Fri, Sat 9:30-5

Photocopy machine. .10/copy (.15 staff-assisted). 7 microfilm readers; 1 reader/printer. Charge varies. Photocopy service via mail honored. Materials do not circulate. No Interlibrary Loan. Holdings: Index to births, marriages, and deaths for City of Providence 1636-1945. Arnold Vital Record 1636-1850. Providence City Directories 1824 to present. Rhode Island Index - Index to "Providence Journal" includes personal name entries for prominent Rhode Island residents.

PROVIDENCE - RHODE ISLAND HISTORICAL SOCIETY LIBRARY
    121 Hope Street   195 East to Gano St. Exit 3. North
    Providence, RI 02906   on Gano to Power St. East on Power
    401-331-8575   to Hope St. On-street parking is
    Closed Mondays in winter   plentiful.
    Tues 9-5 reading room only
    Wed, Sat 9-6
    Summer Hours: Mon 12-9; Tues-Thurs 9-6; Fri 9-5 reading room only.

No fees. Registration forms to fill out, then a library card will be issued. Purses and packages must be checked in lockers. Photocopy machine, .10/copy. 4 microfilm readers; 2 reader/printers. .35/copy. $7 charge for answering genealogical letters. Includes 4 photocopies. List of Professional Genealogists sent upon request. Materials do not circulate. No Interlibrary Loan. Holdings: Federal and State Census Records (including complete 1880 & 1900 Soundex Index). Gravestone records, manuscripts, over 12,000 bound volumes with 6,000 names represented. War and pension records, indexed. Complete R. I. newspapers. Friends Quaker Meeting records for all New England. (Monthly Meetings contain vital records.) From as early as 1600s to 1900s. On microfilm (172 reels).

PROVIDENCE - RHODE ISLAND STATE ARCHIVES
    Room 43. State House   State House exit, Rte 94. Metered
    Providence, RI 02903   on-street parking. Parking lots
    401-277-2353   available when legislature not in
    Mon-Fri 9-4:30   session (June 1-Dec 31)

No research fees. Identification must be presented. Materials do not circulate. Best to call ahead to make appointment. Staff-operated photocopying, .50/copy. 1 microfilm reader. Service by mail. Charge only for copies and postage. Holdings: Census Records (state and federal), Military records - Colonial Wars, Revolutionary War, War of 1812. Petitions to General Assembly, basic correspondence. There is a card catalog and index of Revolutionary and Civil War files. Most material was microfilmed by the Mormon Church. Holdings also include Arnold's Vital Record.

RHODE ISLAND

WESTERLY - <u>WESTERLY PUBLIC LIBRARY</u>
Broad Street   Downtown Westerly, next to Wilcox Park.
Westerly, RI 02891   On-street parking and municipal
401-596-2877   parking lots.
Mon, Tues, Wed, 8 a.m. - 9 p.m.
Thurs & Fri, 8-5; Sat 8-3
(closed Sat, July and August)

Photocopy machine .15/copy. 2 microfilm readers; 1 reader/printer, .35/copy.
Letters answered. Basic research only. Extensive searching not done.
Materials do not circulate. No Interlibrary Loan. <u>Holdings</u>: Rhode Island and
Connecticut genealogies. Many unique family genealogies for the Westerly area
(includes some towns in Connecticut). Clippings, manuscripts, local newspaper
index, Westerly Vital Statistics. Fee charged for research by mail done for
out-of-state residents. Amount varies. (Minimum $5 includes 5 photocopies and
postage.)

WOONSOCKET - <u>UNION SAINT-JEAN BAPTISTE BIBLIOTHEQUE MALLET</u>
One Social Street   Near Woonsocket Public Library
Woonsocket, RI 02895   and the Post Office. No parking
401-769-0520   facilities.
Mon-Fri 8-4:30

No fees. No photocopy machine. Can use Post Office copying facilities. 1
microfilm reader. Letters answered. Does not help with genealogy research.
Materials do not circulate. No Interlibrary Loan. <u>Holdings</u>: French-Canadian
Genealogy. Old French newspapers on microfilm. Vertical File material on
French-Canadians in the U.S. Photograph file. Parish histories.

****

SOCIETIES

<u>AMERICAN FRENCH GENEALOGICAL SOCIETY</u>   Robert Quintin, President
P.O. Box 2113   28 Felsmere Avenue
Pawtucket, RI 02861   Pawtucket, RI 02861
                            401-723-6797

Founded February 1978 "to discover, preserve and study Franco-American
Heritage." Membership requirement: Must be French-Canadian or French. Dues:
$10 per year individual. Meetings: Monthly except April, June, July, August
and December. Held at LeFoyer, 151 Fountain Ave., Pawtucket. Last Wed of
month. Guest speakers. Also weekly research sessions, Tues 7-11 p.m.

<u>LIBRARY</u> of 1,000 volumes at LeFoyer (a social club) open only to Society
members. Members of the Society will do genealogical research for $25 per
family name searched. If no information is found the money is refunded. Use
Society mailing address.

<u>PUBLICATION</u>: "Je me souviens" (quarterly) 60 pages per issue. Available only
with society membership. Back copies available $2.50 per issue stapled, $3.50
bound.

RHODE ISLAND BLACK HERITAGE SOCIETY
        45 Hamilton Street   Off Broad Street, ten minutes from
        Providence, RI 02907   downtown. On-street parking only.
        401-461-5340

Founded 1975 "for researching, documenting, collecting and exhibiting materials
relating to all periods of black life in Rhode Island." Membership open to all.
Dues: $15 individual, $3 student. Location of meetings vary. Annual meeting
in December.

LIBRARY of 1,000 volumes. Family collections, photographs, seamen's records.
Mon-Fri 9-4:30. No fee. Photocopy machine .05/copy. One microfilm reader.
Research by mail. Materials do not circulate. Interlibrary Loan honored.

PUBLICATION: Newsletter starting December, 1979.

RHODE ISLAND GENEALOGICAL SOCIETY
        P.O. Box 7618   Jane Fletcher Fiske, F.A.S.G., Pres.
        Warwick, RI 02887-7618   44 Stonecleave Road
                                              Boxford, MA 01921

Founded 1975 to bring together genealogists, historians, and others interested
in accurate genealogical research, to encourage preservation of genealogical
records, to conduct workshops in the field of genealogy, and to publish
genealogical materials. Membership open to all. Dues: $8 per year individual.
$12 per couple. Meetings 4-6 times a year. Location varies.

PUBLICATION: Rhode Island Roots (Quarterly) Available only with membership.
Mrs. Mildred M. Chamberlain, Editor. Queries of 30 words or less, $5 to non-
members, $3 to members. Articles welcome. First issue 1975-1979, $3.75. Peleg
Burrough's Journal 1778-1798, includes births, marriages and deaths in Little
Compton and Tiverton, RI. $19 postpaid from RIGS, 128 Massasoit Drive, Warwick,
RI 02888.

RHODE ISLAND JEWISH HISTORICAL ASSOCIATION
        130 Sessions Street   Eleanor F. Horvitz
        Providence, RI 02906   Librarian Archivist
        401-331-1360   20 Alfred Stone Rd.
                                              Providence, RI 02906
                                              401-521-9348

Founded 1951 "to procure, collect and preserve books, records, etc. . . and any
historical material relating to the history of the Jews of Rhode Island; to
encourage and promote the study of such history . . . and to publish information
as to such history." Membership open to all. Dues: $20 per year. One annual
meeting in the spring and one interim winter meeting - both at the Jewish
Community Center, Elmgrove Avenue, Providence, Rhode Island.

PUBLICATION: <u>Rhode Island Jewish Historical Notes</u>. Free with membership. $10 per issue otherwise. George C. Kellner, Editor. Queries accepted. Librarian will do some research. Charge for photocopies. Journal's first issue 1954. Back issues available by individual or by volume (4 issues per volume). Price varies. Out of print issues may be photocopied.

<u>RHODE ISLAND STATE SOCIETY OF THE NSDAR</u> (There are 19 individual chapters)
>   Mrs. Frederick N. Tompkins, Honorary State Regent and Genealogical
>   Records Chairman.
>   10 Marshall Way, Rumford, RI.
>   401-434-8195

Founded ca 1892. Conducts historical, educational and patriotic activities. Membership: Must be direct descendant of Revolutionary War Soldier. Meetings: 8 times per year per chapter. Location of meetings varies. Two statewide meetings per year. Directories and Yearbooks available to members only. No periodical publications at state level. Annual volumes at RIHS, indexed.

<u>SOCIETY OF MAYFLOWER DESCENDANTS</u>
>   Mrs. Harold P. Williams, Secretary
>   35 Hodsell Street, Cranston, RI 02910
>   401-467-7594

Founded 1901 "To perpetuate the memory of the pilgrims and to publish genealogical and historical information relating to the pilgrims." Membership: Proven descent from a passenger on the Mayflower. Dues: $9 per year. Meetings: 4 per year. Location varies.

PUBLICATION: "Mayflower Newsletter." Available only to members. Mrs. Harold J. Hubbard, Editor. First Issue 1958.

****

PERIODICALS

<u>THE AMERICAN GENEALOGIST</u>
Dept. H, 128 Massasoit Drive   Owner/Editor: Ruth Wilder Sherman, F.A.S.G.
Warwick, RI 02888   Associate Editor: David L. Greene, F.A.S.G.

An independent quarterly journal, dedicated to the elevation of genealogical scholarship, through carefully documented analyses of genealogical problems and through short compiled genealogies. Founded 1922 by Donald Lines Jacobus. Subscription: $15 (US) annually.

RHODE ISLAND GENEALOGICAL REGISTER
    P.O. Box 585   Owner/Editor: Alden G. Beaman
    East Princeton, Mass.
    01517

An independent journal of 96 pages per issue. Contains Will Abstracts of all
cities & towns incorporated before 1850; Land Evidence Abstracts; Court of
Common Pleas Abstracts; Cemetery Records; Town Council Records; Rhode Island
Families and Persons who left Rhode Island. Volume 1 1977. Dates vary; approximately two volumes per year. 10 volumes to date (1984). Prices: $25-$40 per
volume.

****

BOOKS AND ARTICLES

Farnham, Charles W. "Rhode Island Colonial Records," in Rhode Island History.
    Vol. 29, Numbers 1 and 2. (Reprints available from R.I. Hist. Soc. Library)

Fiske, Jane F. "Genealogical Research in Rhode Island," in New England
    Historical and Genealogical Register, July, 1982, and in Genealogical Re-
    search in New England, Genealogical Publishing Co., 1984.

Lamar, Christine. A Guide to Genealogical Materials at the Rhode Island
    Historical Society Library. 1984.

Tarte, Robert J. Your Genealogical Heritage, Providence, RI. Rhode Island
    Bicentennial Commission, 1975.

****

VERMONT

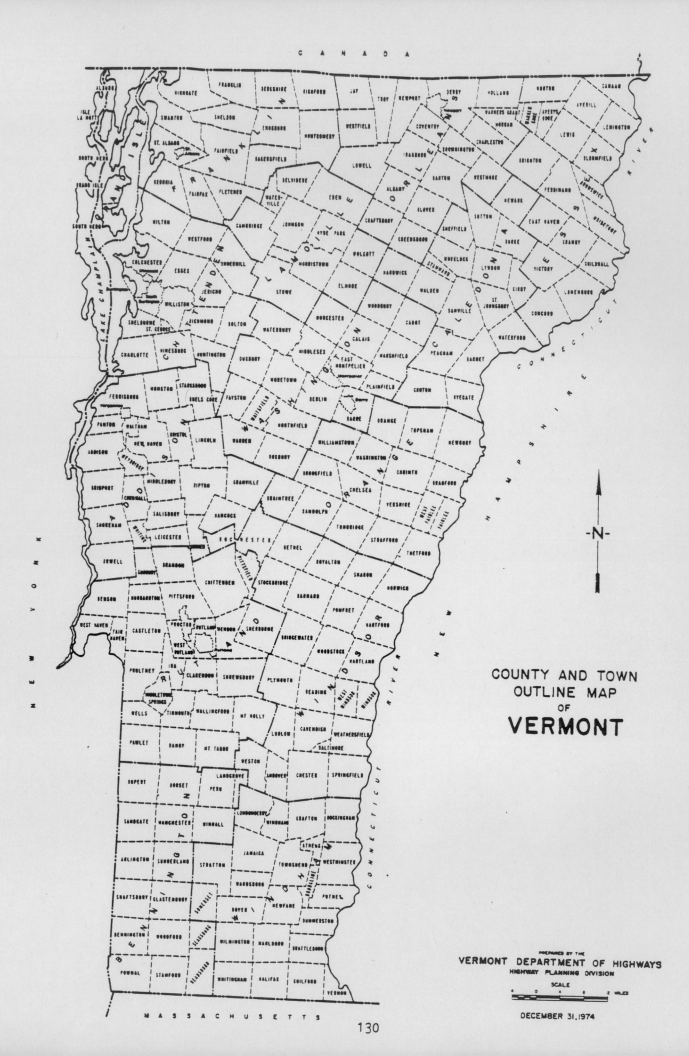

COUNTY AND TOWN
OUTLINE MAP
OF
VERMONT

-N-

PREPARED BY THE
VERMONT DEPARTMENT OF HIGHWAYS
HIGHWAY PLANNING DIVISION

SCALE

DECEMBER 31, 1974

130

VERMONT

Vermont was the last New England state to be opened up to settlement. Permanent substantial settlements were first made in the 1760s under New Hampshire charters and by 1777 were sufficiently numerous to establish an independent government. From 1765 to 1791 the area was in dispute between the settlers in the New Hampshire Grants and the patentees, as well as the authority of New York to which jurisdiction had been assigned by the crown. A man whose address is given as Gloucester County, New York or Cumberland County, New York, in the 1770s was actually living in present day Vermont. In 1791 Vermont was finally recognized and admitted to the Union as the fourteenth state.

Although there was a tendency for settlers from New Hampshire and eastern Massachusetts and Connecticut to settle east of the Green Mountains, and for those from western Connecticut and Massachusetts and New York state to move up the west side, these trends cannot be relied upon. There are families of Allens, Clarks, Smiths, Baileys, Chamberlains, Johnsons, etc. in all parts of the state from every other New England state. Only a small percentage of the Allens living in Vermont by 1800 were related to Ethan and Ira. From the earliest days of settlement, but in large numbers after the Civil War, people of French ancestry from the province of Quebec have entered Vermont to become an important element of the population. Other immigrant groups from Europe were as likely to have made their way into Vermont via Canada (especially the port of Montreal) as through Boston or New York. This is especially true of the Irish settlers, 1820-1860. There are also special pockets of settlement, such as the Scots farmers from west and south of Glasgow who established Barnet and Ryegate in 1772.

****

In Vermont the basic unit for genealogical research is the town, much as in Connecticut. The original vital records and recorded copies of deeds remain in the custody of the town clerks. However, the most useful advice for genealogists is - Go first to Montpelier. With two major libraries and other depositories of records and copies of records in a two-block area, a great deal may be accomplished on a single trip to the city on a regular business day.

****

VITAL RECORDS - 1764-1954

VITAL RECORDS
STATE OF VERMONT
PUBLIC RECORDS DIVISION
State Administration Bldg
Montpelier, VT 05602
802-828-3286
Mon-Fri 8-12, 1-4

Directions: Exit 8 from I-89. Left at 1st light (Rte 2). Cross bridge and right at next light (State St). 3d building on left - small building behind parking lot of 133 State St., marked "Vital Records," across from the Vermont Travel Bureau.

Holdings: Index to state-wide vital records, 1764-1954. On cards, open to public. Certified copies: $3. Service by mail: $2 search charge which will be credited toward a certified copy if anything is found.

VITAL RECORDS - 1955 TO PRESENT

VITAL RECORDS
60 Main Street, P.O. Box 70
Burlington, VT 05402
802-863-7275
Mon-Fri 8-12 and 1-4 excluding
    holidays

Directions: Exit 14W from I-89, go
straight, past University of Vermont down
Main Street. Lake Champlain can be seen
as you head down the hill. 60 Main St
is a large brick building, on the right,
almost to the lake.

Holdings: Births, marriages, and deaths since 1955. Divorces since 1968.
Staff retrieves records, 5 at a time. Certified copies: $3. Service by mail:
$2 search charge which will be credited toward a certified copy if anything is
found.

****

    The list of Vermont Towns given below is taken from Vermont Place Names:
Footprints of History, by Esther Swift. The dates are the original grant dates.
Letters in parentheses are used for divided counties, as follows:

Bennington (N) = Bennington County, North District;
Bennington (S) = Bennington County, South District;
Orange (B) = Orange County, Bradford District;
Orange (R) = Orange County, Randolph District;
Rutland (F.H.) = Rutland County, Fair Haven District;
Rutland (R) = Rutland County, Rutland District;
Windham (M) = Windham County, Marlboro District;
Windham (W) = Windham County, Westminster District;
Windsor (H) = Windsor County, Hartford District;
Windsor (W) = Windsor County, Windsor District.

TOWN	GRANT DATE	COUNTY	TOWN	GRANT DATE	COUNTY
Addison	1761	Addison	Bolton	1763	Chittenden
Albany	1782	Orleans	Bradford	1770	Orange (B)
Alburg	1781	Grand Isle	Braintree	1781	Orange (R)
Andover	1761	Windsor (W)	Brandon	1761	Rutland (R)
Arlington	1761	Bennington (N)	Brattleboro	1753	Windham (M)
Athens	1780	Windham (W)	Bridport	1761	Addison
Averill	1762	Essex	Bridgewater	1761	Windsor (H)
Averys Gore	1791	Essex	Brighton	1781	Essex
Bakersfield	1791	Franklin	Bristol	1761	Addison
Baltimore	1793	Windsor (W)	Brookfield	1781	Orange (R)
Barnard	1761	Windsor (H)	Brookline	1794	Windham (W)
Barnet	1763	Caledonia	Brownington	1790	Orleans
Barre	1781	Washington	Brunswick	1761	Essex
Barton	1789	Orleans	Buels Gore	1780	Chittenden
Belvidere	1791	Lamoille	Burke	1782	Caledonia
Bennington	1749/50	Bennington (S)	Burlington	1763	Chittenden
Benson	1780	Rutland (F.H.)	Cabot	1780	Washington
Berkshire	1781	Franklin	Calais	1781	Washington
Berlin	1763	Washington	Cambridge	1781	Lamoille
Bethel	1779	Windsor (H)	Canaan	1782	Essex
Bloomfield	1762	Essex	Castleton	1761	Rutland (F.H.)

TOWN	GRANT DATE	COUNTY	TOWN	GRANT DATE	COUNTY
Cavendish	1761	Windsor (W)	Hinesburg	1762	Chittenden
Charleston	1780	Orleans	Holland	1779	Orleans
Charlotte	1762	Chittenden	Hubbardton	1764	Rutland (F.H.)
Chelsea	1781	Orange (R)	Huntington	1763	Chittenden
Chester	1754	Windsor (W)	Hyde Park	1781	Lamoille
Chittenden	1780	Rutland (R)	Ira	1781	Rutland (R)
Clarendon	1761	Rutland (R)	Irasburg	1781	Orleans
Colchester	1763	Chittenden	Isles La Motte	1779	Grand Isle
Concord	1780	Essex	Jamaica	1780	Windham (W)
Corinth	1764	Orange (B)	Jay	1792	Orleans
Cornwall	1761	Addison	Jericho	1763	Chittenden
Coventry	1780	Orleans	Johnson	1792	Lamoille
Craftsbury	1781	Orleans	Kirby	1807	Caledonia
Danby	1761	Rutland (R)	Landgrove	1780	Bennington (N)
Danville	1786	Caledonia	Leicester	1761	Addison
Derby	1779	Orleans	Lemington	1762	Essex
Dorset	1761	Bennington (N)	Lewis	1762	Essex
Dover	1810	Windham (M)	Lincoln	1780	Addison
Dummerston	1753	Windham (M)	Londonderry	1780	Windham (W)
Duxbury	1763	Washington	Lowell	1791	Orleans
East Haven	1790	Essex	Ludlow	1761	Windsor (W)
East Montpelier	1781	Washington	Lunenburg	1763	Essex
Eden	1781	Lamoille	Lyndon	1780	Caledonia
Elmore	1781	Lamoille	Maidstone	1761	Essex
Enosburg	1780	Franklin	Manchester	1761	Bennington (N)
Essex	1763	Chittenden	Marlboro	1751	Windham (M)
Fair Haven	1779	Rutland (F.H.)	Marshfield	1782	Washington
Fairfax	1763	Franklin	Mendon	1781	Rutland (R)
Fairfield	1763	Franklin	Middlebury	1761	Addison
Fairlee	1761	Orange (B)	Middlesex	1763	Washington
Fayston	1782	Washington	Middletown Springs		
Ferdinand	1761	Essex		1784	Rutland (R)
Ferrisburg	1762	Addison	Milton	1763	Chittenden
Fletcher	1781	Franklin	Monkton	1762	Addison
Franklin	1789	Franklin	Montgomery	1789	Franklin
Georgia	1763	Franklin	Montpelier	1781	Washington
Glastenbury	1761	Bennington (S)	Moretown	1763	Washington
Glover	1783	Orleans	Morgan	1780	Orleans
Goshen	1792	Addison	Morristown	1781	Lamoille
Grafton	1754	Windham (W)	Mount Holly	1792	Rutland (R)
Granby	1761	Essex	Mount Tabor	1761	Rutland (R)
Grand Isle	1779	Grand Isle	New Haven	1761	Addison
Granville	1781	Addison	Newark	1781	Caledonia
Greensboro	1781	Orleans	Newbury	1763	Orange (B)
Groton	1789	Caledonia	Newfane	1753	Windham (M)
Guildhall	1761	Essex	Newport	1802	Orleans
Guilford	1754	Windham (M)	North Hero	1779	Grand Isle
Halifax	1750	Windham (M)	Northfield	1781	Washington
Hancock	1781	Addison	Norton	1779	Essex
Hardwick	1781	Caledonia	Norwich	1761	Windsor (H)
Hartford	1761	Windsor (H)	Orange	1781	Orange (R)
Hartland	1761	Windsor (H)	Orwell	1763	Addison
Highgate	1763	Franklin	Panton	1761	Addison

TOWN	GRANT DATE	COUNTY	TOWN	GRANT DATE	COUNTY
Pawlet	1761	Rutland (F.H.)	Swanton	1763	Franklin
Peacham	1763	Caledonia	Thetford	1761	Orange (B)
Peru	1761	Bennington (N)	Tinmouth	1761	Rutland (R)
Pittsfield	1781	Rutland (R)	Topsham	1763	Orange (B)
Pittsford	1761	Rutland (R)	Townshend	1753	Windham (W)
Plainfield	1797	Washington	Troy	1801	Orleans
Plymouth	1761	Windsor (W)	Tunbridge	1761	Orange (R)
Pomfret	1761	Windsor (H)	Underhill	1763	Chittenden
Poultney	1761	Rutland (F.H.)	Vergennes	1788	Addison
Pownal	1760	Bennington (S)	Vernon	1753	Windham (M)
Proctor	1886	Rutland (R)	Vershire	1781	Orange (B)
Putney	1753	Windham (W)	Victory	1781	Essex
Randolph	1781	Orange (R)	Waitsfield	1782	Washington
Reading	1761	Windsor (W)	Walden	1781	Caledonia
Readsboro	1770	Bennington (S)	Wallingford	1761	Rutland (R)
Richford	1780	Franklin	Waltham	1796	Addison
Richmond	1794	Chittenden	Wardsboro	1780	Windham (M)
Ripton	1781	Addison	Warner's Grant	1791	Essex
Rochester	1781	Windsor (H)	Warren	1780	Washington
Rockingham	1752	Windham (W)	Warren Gore	1789	Essex
Roxbury	1781	Washington	Washington	1781	Orange (R)
Royalton	1769	Windsor (H)	Waterbury	1763	Washington
Rupert	1761	Bennington (N)	Waterford	1780	Caledonia
Rutland	1761	Rutland (R)	Waterville	1824	Lamoille
Ryegate	1763	Caledonia	Weathersfield	1761	Windsor (W)
Saint Albans	1763	Franklin	Wells	1761	Rutland (F.H.)
Saint George	1763	Chittenden	West Fairlee	1797	Orange (B)
Saint Johnsbury	1786	Caledonia	West Haven	1792	Rutland (F.H.)
Salisbury	1761	Addison	West Rutland	1886	Rutland (R)
Sandgate	1761	Bennington (N)	West Windsor	1848	Windsor (W)
Searsburg	1781	Bennington (S)	Westfield	1780	Orleans
Shaftsbury	1761	Bennington (S)	Westford	1763	Chittenden
Sharon	1761	Windsor (H)	Westminster	1752	Windham (W)
Sheffield	1793	Caledonia	Westmore	1781	Orleans
Shelburne	1763	Chittenden	Weston	1799	Windsor (W)
Sheldon	1763	Franklin	Weybridge	1761	Addison
Sherburn	1761	Rutland (R)	Wheelock	1785	Caledonia
Shoreham	1761	Addison	Whiting	1763	Addison
Shrewsbury	1761	Rutland (R)	Whitingham	1770	Windham (M)
Somerset	1761	Windham (M)	Williamstown	1781	Orange (R)
South Burlington	1864	Chittenden	Williston	1763	Chittenden
South Hero	1779	Grand Isle	Wilmington	1751	Windham (M)
Springfield	1761	Windsor (W)	Windham	1795	Windham (W)
Stamford	1753	Bennington (S)	Windsor	1761	Windsor (W)
Stannard	1867	Caledonia	Winhall	1761	Bennington (N)
Starksboro	1780	Addison	Winooski	1921	Chittenden
Stockbridge	1761	Windsor (H)	Wolcott	1781	Lamoille
Stowe	1763	Lamoille	Woodbury	1781	Washington
Strafford	1761	Orange (B)	Woodford	1753	Bennington (S)
Stratton	1761	Windham (M)	Woodstock	1761	Windsor (H)
Sudbury	1763	Rutland (F.H.)	Worcester	1763	Washington
Sunderland	1761	Bennington (N)			
Sutton	1782	Caledonia			

CENSUS RECORDS - FEDERAL

Federal census returns are available for Vermont beginning with the 1790 census, which was actually taken in Vermont in 1791 when Vermont was admitted as the fourteenth state. Federal census returns, 1790-1900, including Soundex Index to 1880 and 1900 are available at the VERMONT DEPARTMENT OF LIBRARIES. LAW AND DOCUMENT UNIT at 111 State Street in Montpelier. (Mailing address: c/o State Office Bldg P.O. Montpelier, VT 05602). Also at NATIONAL ARCHIVES - BOSTON BRANCH in Waltham, Mass. (See Page 71)

CENSUS RECORDS - STATE

There are no state censuses for Vermont, per se. There are, however, very limited census returns for parts of the present state taken in 1771 when Vermont was considered by some as part of New York State.

Gloucester County (Northeastern Vermont). See Documentary History of the State of New York, 1849, vol. 4, pp. 708-709.

Cumberland County (Southeastern Vermont). See Antiquarian Documents copied from the semi-weekly Eagle, Brattleboro, Vermont, Jan. 20, 1850. (Typescript copies are at the Vermont Historical Society Library.)

****

PROBATE RECORDS

Vermont has fourteen counties but nineteen probate districts. (5 southern counties have 2 probate courts each.) Holdings of each court include estates, trust estates, guardianships, name changes, adoptions, relinquishments. The latter two categories are confidential. None of the Vermont probate district offices have microfilm readers or printers. HOWEVER, THE RECORDS PRIOR TO 1850 ARE AVAILABLE ON MICROFILM at the PUBLIC RECORDS DIVISION at 6 Baldwin Street, Montpelier. (See complete description under Vermont - Land Records). Photo-copying charges may vary. At present (June, 1985), for example, it is the policy of the Washington County Probate Court Administration in Montpelier that copying will be done for .05/page where possible. Certification, by statute, is an additional $2/document. Not all probate offices are equipped to do their own photocopying, and charges may vary.

ADDISON COUNTY was established in 1785.

Addison Probate Court
Middlebury, VT 05753
802-388-2612
Mon-Fri 8-4:30
Directions: On Rte 7
   facing Court Square.

Probate Records: 1852 to present.
Earlier records destroyed by fire.
New Haven Probate District Records
1824-1957
Staff-operated photocopying.

BENNINGTON COUNTY was established in 1778. The "South Shire" towns include Bennington, Glastenbury, Pownal, Readsboro, Searsburg, Shaftsbury, Stamford, Woodford; the "North Shire" towns include Arlington, Dorset, Landgrove, Manchester, Peru, Rupert, Sandgate, Sunderland, Winhall,

Bennington District Probate Court
207 South St., P.O. Box 607
Bennington, VT 05201
802-442-2951
Mon-Fri 9-12, 1-4:30
Directions: On Rte 7, one block south of Rte 9

Probate Records: From 1778 to present for "South Shire" towns listed above.
Card Index.
Staff-operated photocopying.

Manchester District Probate Court
Route 7   Box 446
Manchester, VT 05254
802-362-1410
Mon-Fri 9-12:30, 1:30-4:30
Directions: In Manchester Village across from Old Equinox House.

Probate Records: 1764 to present for "North Shire" towns listed above.
Card index.
Staff-operated photocopying.

CALEDONIA COUNTY was established in 1792 from Chittenden and Orange Counties.

Caledonia District Probate Court
27 Main Street
St. Johnsbury, VT 05819
802-748-2003
Mon-Fri 8:00-4:30

Probate Records: Early 1790s to present.
Staff-operated photocopying.

Directions: Junction of Rtes 2 and 5.

CHITTENDEN COUNTY was established in 1787 from Addiston County.

Chittenden Probate Court
175 Main Street   Box 511
Burlington, VT 05402
802-864-7481
Mon-Fri 8:30-4:30
Directions: On Rte 2, corner of Main and Church Streets

Probate Records: 1795 to present.
Records prior to 1900 stored away.
Call ahead for retrieval.
Staff-operated photocopying.

ESSEX COUNTY was established in 1792 from Chittenden and Orange Counties.

Essex District Probate Court
Main Street
Island Pond, VT 05846
802-723-4770
Mon-Fri 8:30-12, 1-3:30
Directions: In Town Municipal Building over Community National Bank.

Probate Records: From 1830 to present.
Indexes. Some prior record volumes missing. Others kept in county courthouse in Guildhall. Not readily available.
Staff-operated photocopying.

VERMONT

FRANKLIN COUNTY was established in 1792 from Chittenden County.

Franklin District Probate Court
Church Street
St. Albans, VT 05478
802-524-4112
Mon-Fri By appointment only.
Directions: On Taylor Park, one block east of Rte 7.

Probate Records: 1791 to present.
Card index. Records open to public
but must climb high ladders.
No photocopying available.

GRAND ISLE COUNTY was established in 1802 from Franklin and Chittenden Counties.

Grand Isle District Probate Court
North Hero, VT 05474
802-372-5905
Mon-Fri 8-4:30
Directions: Gray stone building on Main Street (Rte 2)

Probate Records: From early 1800s
to present.
Staff-operated photocopying.

LAMOILLE COUNTY was established in 1835 from Chittenden, Orleans, Franklin and Washington Counties.

Lamoille Probate Court
Hyde Park, VT 05665
802-888-3306
Mon-Fri 8-12, 1-4:30
Directions: Red brick building in center of town.

Probate Records: 1837 to present.
Staff-operated photocopying.

ORANGE COUNTY was established in 1781. The Randolph District Probate Court includes Braintree, Brookfield, Chelsea, Orange, Randolph, Tunbridge, Washington, Williamstown. The Bradford District Probate Court includes Bradford, Corinth, Fairlee, Newbury, Strafford, Thetford, Topsham, Vershire, West Fairlee.

Randolph District Probate Court
Orange County Court House
Chelsea, VT 05038
802-685-4610
Mon-Fri 8-12, 1-4:30
Directions: On Rte 110

Probate Records: 1700s to present,
for towns listed above in Randolph
District. Prior to 1900, only recorded
volumes may be consulted.
Staff-operated photocopying.

Bradford District Probate Court
Wells River, VT 05081
802-757-2351
Mon-Fri 8:30-12, 1-5
Directions: On Rte 5

Probate Records: 1781 to present,
for towns listed above in Bradford
District. Card index.
Staff-operated photocopying.

ORLEANS COUNTY was established in 1792 from Chittenden and Orange Counties.

Orleans District Probate Court
Newport, VT 05855
802-334-8515
Mon-Fri 8-12, 1-4
Directions: Main Street (Rte 5)

Probate Records: 1796 to present.
Prior to 1850, only recorded volumes
may be consulted.
Staff-operated photocopying.

RUTLAND COUNTY was established in 1781 from Bennington County. The Rutland District Probate Court includes Brandon, Chittenden, Clarendon, Danby, Ira, Mendon, Middletown Springs, Mount Holly, Mount Tabor, Pittsfield, Pittsford, Proctor, Rutland, Sherburne, Shrewsbury, Tinmouth, Wallingford, West Rutland; The Fair Haven District Probate Court includes Benson, Castleton, Fair Haven, Hubbardton, Pawlet, Poultney, Sudbury, Wells, West Haven.

Rutland District Probate Court
83 Center St., P.O. Box 339
Rutland, VT 05701
802-775-0114
Mon-Fri 8-4:30
Directions: South on Rte 7 to Center St. Courthouse at Center and Court.

Probate Records: Late 1700s to present. for towns listed in Rutland District. Staff-operated photocopying.

Fair Haven District Probate Court
Fair Haven, VT 05743
802-265-3380
Mon-Fri 8-12, 1-4
Directions: On 22-A in same building as fire station.

Probate Records: Ca. 1800 to present for towns listed above in Fair Haven District. Photocopying available $.25/sheet.

WASHINGTON COUNTY was established in 1810 from Addison, Caledonia, Chittenden and Orange Counties.

Washington District Probate Court
State & Elm Streets, P.O. Box 15
Montpelier, VT 05602
802-223-3405
Mon-Fri 7:45-12, 1-4:30
Directions: Exit 8 from I-89. Left on Taylor. Cross bridge. Right on State Street

Probate Records: 1811 to present. All record volumes salvaged from 1927 flood and restored. Staff-operated photocopying. If material cannot be photocopied, it will be transcribed at $.60/folio.

WINDHAM COUNTY was established in 1781. Marlboro District Probate Court includes Brattleboro, Dover, Dummerston, Guilford, Halifax, Marlboro, Newfane, Somerset, Stratton, Vernon, Wardsboro, Whitingham, Wilmington; The Westminster District Probate Court includes Athens, Brookline, Grafton, Jamaica, Londonderry, Putney, Rockingham, Townshend, Westminster, Windham.

Marlboro District Probate Court
West River Road, P.O. Box 523
Brattleboro, VT 05301
802-254-9700, & 257-7870
Mon-Fri 8-12, 1-5
Directions: on Rte 30, 2 miles north of town. In Brattleboro Professional Center.

Probate Records: 1781 to present for Marlboro District towns listed above. Early original files (up to 1896) are fragile & are stored at Court House in Newfane. Recorded volumes must be used. Staff-operated photocopying.

Westminster District Probate Court
39 Square P.O. Box 47
Bellows Falls, VT 05101
802-463-3019
Mon-Fri 8-12, 1-4:30
Directions: Junction Rtes 5 & 12. Second floor.

Probate records: from 1781 to present. Early original files are fragile and recorded volumes must be used. Staff-operated photocopying.

WINDSOR COUNTY was established in 1781. The <u>Windsor District Probate Court</u> includes Andover, Baltimore, Cavendish, Chester, Ludlow, Plymouth, Reading, Springfield, Weathersfield, West Windsor, Weston, <u>Windsor</u>; <u>The Hartford District Probate Court</u> includes Barnard, Bethel, Bridgewater, Hartford, Hartland, Norwich, Pomfret, Rochester, Royalton, Sharon, Stockbridge, <u>Woodstock.</u>

<u>Windsor District Probate Court</u>
2 Main Street   P.O. Box 402
North Springfield, VT 05150
802-886-2284
Mon-Fri 8-4:30
Directions: 3 miles from center of Springfield, 1st bldg on left on 1st left-hand turn beyond Idlenot Dairy Plant (off Rte 106)

Probate Records: Late 1700s to present, for Windsor District towns listed above. Original files before 1900 in storage. Must use recorded volumes. Staff-operated photocopying. Small charge. Call ahead. Room used for other purposes Usually unavailable Tues. mornings.

<u>Hartford District Probate Court</u>
On the Green
Woodstock, VT 05091
802-457-1503
Mon-Fri 8-12, 1-4:30
Directions: Center of Woodstock facing green.

Probate Records: 1783 to present. For early records, only recorded volumes may be consulted. Staff-operated photocopying

****

LAND RECORDS

In Vermont, the original jurisdiction over land records (ownership and transfer of property) is with the local town or city clerk. However, Land Records up to 1850, for the entire state, are available on microfilm at the <u>State of Vermont Public Records Division</u>, 6 Baldwin Street, Montpelier. These land records were microfilmed by the Mormon Church microfilming project, and are therefore also available through any of the LDS Branch Libraries. (See listing under each state.) For Land Records after 1850, the individual town or city clerk's office must be consulted.

<u>STATE OF VERMONT</u>
<u>PUBLIC RECORDS DIVISION</u>
6 Baldwin Street
Montpelier, VT 05602
(Mailing address: 133 State St.)
802-828-3288
Mon-Fri 7:45-4

Directions: Exit 8 from I-89. Left at 1st light (Rte 2). Cross bridge and right at next light (State St.). On left is insurance company & large grey State Office Building. Public Records is yellow building at back of State parking lot. Park in lot.

Holdings: <u>All records on microfilm and all open to the public</u>. Town records to 1850 as microfilmed by the Mormons. Includes land records, town meeting records, vital records, etc. Probate records up to 1850. Barbour Index to Connecticut Vital Records. Church and cemetery records from various sources. 6 microfilm readers; 2 reader/printers. Printouts: 12 X 18 $1; 18 X 24 $2.

****

CEMETERY RECORDS

THE VERMONT OLD CEMETERY ASSOCIATION (VOCA), founded in 1958, is dedicated to the restoration and preservation of old and abandoned cemeteries. Cemetery transcriptions are sparse but the Association will share what they have if you mention the specific town. Membership of $1 includes a quarterly newsletter which contains information on cemeteries being restored and occasionally cemeteries which have been transcribed. Please address all correspondence to: Vickie Harlow, 26 Robinson Pkwy., Burlington, VT 05401.

THE GENEALOGICAL SOCIETY OF VERMONT often publishes copies of cemetery records in its quarterly, "Branches and Twigs." (See description under VERMONT - SOCIETIES)

THE VERMONT HISTORICAL SOCIETY has many printed and manuscript cemetery records, including those collected by the D.A.R. chapters. (See description under VERMONT - SOCIETIES)

****

CHURCH RECORDS

Vermont church records, including records of baptism, marriage, death, membership, are usually found at the local level. They may be kept in church offices, parsonages, homes of church clerks, or town office vaults. During the years 1938-42, the Vermont Historical Records Survey of the W.P.A. worked towards completion of an inventory of the church records of Vermont. The aim was to discover and describe all existing church records and to give the location of the records at the time of the inventory. However, only three books were actually published:

   Inventory of the Church Archives of Vermont: Churches of Hinesburg: A Preliminary publication.

   Directory of Churches and Religious Organizations in the State of Vermont. 1939.

   Inventory of the Church Archives of Vermont, No. 1. The Diocese of Vermont Protestant Episcopal. 1940.

The material for other inventories which was collected but not published is now located at the VERMONT PUBLIC RECORDS DIVISION in Montpelier. Even though the material is forty years old, it is helpful in discovering what sorts of records were available and where they were then located. From 1970-1975, the National Society of the Colonial Dames in Vermont attempted to discover the church records that are not included in the W.P.A. survey. The list of their findings is at the Public Records Division also.

BAPTIST   VERMONT BAPTIST STATE CONVENTION
                   19 Orchard Terrace   P.O. Box 188   Mon-Fri
                   Burlington, VT 05402 802-863-6308   8-4:30

The Baptist Convention Archives for Vermont are at the Bailey/Howe Library of The University of Vermont. Inquirers may also be referred to other depositories such as the Vermont Historical Society, etc., or to local church clerks. The

Baptist State Convention does not keep records. They encourage local church clerks to deposit their early records where they can be preserved and cared for, but this is not always done. An inquirer may also be referred to the American Baptist Historical Society in Rochester, N.Y.

CATHOLIC

ARCHIVES OF THE ROMAN CATHOLIC DIOCESE OF BURLINGTON
351 North Avenue   Wed & Thurs
Burlington, VT 05401   By appointment only
802-658-6110

Inquiries by mail are answered, but genealogical requests in most cases are referred to the appropriate parish which should have custody of the records. A few early record books are in the Archives; they are indexed, but provide very little collateral information, e.g., place of birth. Referrals are practical only if a town, or at least county, in Vermont and approximate date can be provided. The U. S. census is a good preliminary source before writing the Archives. In the early 19th century priests from Canada and Massachusetts served the Catholics in Vermont, often carrying their records with them. Current locations of these records are not available through this office. The Archives holds the inactive records of the administration of this Diocese, covering the state of Vermont, from its establishment in 1853, deceased bishops' and priests' papers, parish and institutional historical files, etc., as well as a large variety of non-sacramental parish record books.

CONGREGATIONAL   (See: UNITED CHURCH OF CHRIST)

EPISCOPALIAN

EPISCOPAL DIOCESAN CENTER
Rock Point
Burlington, VT 05401   802-863-3431

Archives are in the custody of Special Collections, Bailey/Howe Library of the University of Vermont.

METHODIST

TROY ANNUAL CONFERENCE OF THE UNITED METHODIST CHURCH
3 Riverside Drive
Fultonville, NY 12072   518-853-3311

Chief genealogical help would be in regard to the clergy during the time they were in the conference. Sources are the set of Journals of the Vermont Methodist Conference and Methodist Episcopal Church and the year books of the Troy Conference. The archives of the conference are at the Green Mountain College Library. (See description under VERMONT - LIBRARIES)

UNITED CHURCH OF CHRIST   VERMONT CONFERENCE UNITED CHURCH OF CHRIST
285 Maple Street   802-864-0248
Burlington, VT 05401   Mon-Fri 9-5

No church records. Chief service to genealogists is information regarding a minister's time and place of service. Contact local churches and the Congregational Library in Boston for vital statistics. (See description under MASSACHUSETTS - CHURCH RECORDS.)

(For addresses of other denominations, see latest VERMONT YEARBOOK.)

****

MILITARY RECORDS

VERMONT ADJUTANT GENERAL   Directions: Exit 8 from I-89. At
Veterans Affairs Office   first light, turn left. Cross bridge.
118 State Street   At first light, turn right. Office
Montpelier, VT 05602   is small white house at back of parking
802-828-3381   lot on right 1/2 way down block.
Mon-Fri 7:45-4:30

Holdings include Printed War Rosters plus card files for:
    Graves registration of veterans, begun by W.P.A. and kept up-to-date.
    Veterans' service files beginning with Revolutionary War.
    State Militia and National Guard files from pre-revolutionary times to 1950.
National Guard personnel files (actual records) 1946-1968. After 1968, these files are at the Military Personnel Records Office, Camp Johnson, Winooski, VT. Most original records before 1920, such as muster rolls, pay rolls, etc. were destroyed by fire in 1945. Files are not open to the public. However, the staff makes every effort to answer questions, subject to the Privacy Act of 1974. Mail inquiries will be answered.

****

LIBRARIES

There are 218 public libraries in Vermont. Their holdings vary greatly. The majority of them have small collections which may include items of genealogical interest. Many are open 12 hours a week or less and do not have staff to do any research. For a list of all libraries, consult the Vermont Library Directory at any large Vermont library, or the American Library Directory in most large libraries, to see what is available and what hours of service are offered.

BARRE - ALDRICH PUBLIC LIBRARY
Washington, Corner of Elm St.   On U.S. 302 at junction of Vt 14.
P.O. Box 453, Barre, VT 05641
802-476-7550
Mon, Tues, Wed, Fri 12-8; Thurs, 10-8; Sat 9-12

Photocopying at modest fee. 1 microfilm reader. Arrangements for printouts can be made through the Public Records Division. Mail inquiries not encouraged. Basic holdings: General Vermont reference material and some family genealogies. A great deal of material on Barre and Barre families. An important photographic collection which includes family pictures, school and other group pictures.

BRATTLEBORO - BROOKS MEMORIAL LIBRARY
224 Main Street   Next door to Municipal Center.
Brattleboro, VT 05301   Parking in rear, and a rear
802-254-5290   entrance to library.
Mon-Fri 9-9; Sat 9-5 (exc summer, 9-12)

Self service photocopying $.10/copy. Microfilm reader and print out, $.10/copy.
Staff research is limited. Mail is answered. No loans. One must sign in at
desk and get key to use locked room. Holdings include a good basic genealogical
reference collection for New England with stress on Vermont and Massachusetts.
Also census 1830-1900 for Windham County, 2 Brattleboro newspapers, small
collection of family histories. There is a separate room for local history.

BENNINGTON - GENEALOGICAL LIBRARY OF BENNINGTON MUSEUM
Bennington, VT 05201   West of Route 9 from the center
802-447-1571   of town on the left in the
Mon-Fri 9-12 noon   Bennington Museum.
(Hours may vary)
Closed Sat., Sun. Closed Dec., Jan., Feb.

The museum entrance fee is charged for the first admittance in any one trip. A
courtesy card is issued for re-entrance. A one-year membership carries
unlimited museum and library privileges for one person for one year. Limited
photocopying by staff. $.25 per copy. No microfilm. No loans. A fee schedule
is set for research services by mail. Concentration is on the local area; does
not include all of New England.

BURLINGTON - FLETCHER FREE LIBRARY
235 College Street   From U.S. 7 (Willard St.) turn
Burlington, VT 05401   west onto College St. Library is
802-863-3403   on corner of College St. and S.
Mon & Wed 8:30-9   Winooski Avenue.
Tues, Thurs, Fri 8:30-6; Sat 9-5:30
(Sun 2-5, Oct - Mar only)

Photocopying self-service $.10/page. 2 microfilm reader/printers. 1 microfiche
reader. Circulating material to card-holders only. (Non-resident fee:
$15/year) Interlibrary loan honored using standard ILL procedures. Basic
holdings: Miscellaneous genealogical collection (several hundred books) includes Vermont Military Rosters, NEHGS "Register" vols. 1-date, index to
Burlington birth, death and marriage records 1789-1833, index to Burlington
marriages 1830-1963. Local History Collection includes Burlington City
Directories and Annual Reports from about 1870, Vermont town and county
histories, Beers Atlases, Hemenway. Genealogical Sources in the Reference
Department of the Fletcher Free Library (annotated bibliography) available for
$1.50 prepaid.

BURLINGTON - <u>BAILEY/HOWE LIBRARY</u>   <u>UNIVERSITY OF VERMONT</u>

Burlington, VT 05405   Adjacent to U.S. 2 between I-89
802-656-2020   and downtown Burlington. Library
Ref. Tel. 802-656-2022   is north of Rte 2 and east of
Mon-Fri 8 a.m. to 12 p.m.   common.
Sat 9 a.m. to 11 p.m.
Sun 9 a.m. to 12 p.m.   Hours for school term only.
During summer session, Library closes at 10 Mon-Thurs. 5 on Fri &
Sat. Open Sun 6-10. At Intersession, library closes at 5 Mon-Fri,
all day Sat., Sun.

Self-service photocopying. Several machines. $.05/page. 15 or more microfilm
readers. Printout service available. Good staffing. No genealogical research
done except for quick check of specific items. Staff will send names of researchers if requested. Materials in circulation collection are loaned to autho-
rized borrowers: students, faculty, staff and residents of Burlington and
certain Chittenden County towns. Interlibrary loan to other libraries using
standard ILL forms. The library has a large collection of Vermontiana; considerable material on other New England States; material on Canadian local history
and genealogy; a small number of family histories; newspapers on microfilm,
including Burlington Free Press; and several indexing tools going back to 1827
and including death notices.

   <u>SPECIAL</u> <u>COLLECTIONS</u> <u>OF</u> <u>THE</u> <u>UNIVERSITY</u> <u>OF</u> <u>VERMONT</u> <u>LIBRARY</u>
          School terms: Mon-Thur 8:30 a.m. - 9 p.m.
                         Fri 8:30 a.m. - 5 p.m.; Sat 9 - 12 noon.
          Intersession: 8:30 a.m. - 5 p.m.

Photocopying available with staff approval. Good staffing; very helpful to
visitors. Rare Interlibrary Loan. Holdings include: The Wilbur Collection of
Vermontiana and large manuscript collection; Baptist Church records from around
the state; records of several Burlington area churches; account books; diaries;
letters; town reports; some Vermont Old Cemetery Association transcripts of
inscriptions; many Burlington city school records and the records of a number of
Vermont organizations and societies, including the Vermont Medical Society; a
photograph collection. Visitors should phone or write ahead when planning to
use the manuscript collection as much of it is in special storage in an off-
campus location.

MIDDLEBURY - <u>SHELDON MUSEUM</u>

1 Park Street, Box 126   Museum fronts on small park
Middlebury, VT 05753
802-288-2117
Summer: Mon-Fri, 10-5
Winter: Mon, Wed, Fri 10-5; Tues, Thurs 1-5; some evenings.

Some photocopying. All mail answered. Small amount of research done. No
loans. Holdings include a few family histories and town histories for Addison
county area. Middlebury newspapers from 1801 to present. Not indexed and
request for search must include date. Walton's Registers, Henry Sheldon's
scrapbooks; collection of business manuscripts which includes some names; 19th
century letters, most of them indexed by name; photographs.

MONTPELIER - <u>MONTPELIER VERMONT STAKE, BRANCH GENEALOGICAL LIBRARY</u>

P.O. Box 247   The library is located in the
Montpelier, VT 05602   Montpelier, VT Chapel, Hersey
802-229-0482   Road, <u>Berlin</u>, VT. From
Wed 10-3; Thurs, Fri 6-10   Montpelier, go south toward Barre
Sat 10-3   1 mile. (Rte 302) Blind right on
                                      Hersey Rd. just beyond Wayside
                                      Restaurant.

Open to public. Researchers consult guides and microfilm indexes to locate
specific films of interest. Films are ordered for 2 weeks use at the library.
($2 plus .25 postage) or 6 months ($3 plus .25 postage) Patrons are notified
when items arrive and must come to library to use. 4 microfilm readers and 4
microfiche readers. IGI fiche, CLC on fiche & AIS 1790-1850 census indices on
fiche.

MONTPELIER - <u>VERMONT DEPARTMENT OF LIBRARIES: LAW AND DOCUMENTS DIVISION</u>

111 State Street   From I-89 take exit 8. Left on
Montpelier, VT 05602   Bailey (Rte 2). Cross bridge.
802-828-3268   At light, turn right onto State
Mon-Fri 7:45-4:30   St. Library is in Supreme Court
                                      Building to right of Capitol.

This is a circulating library for Vermont residents. Photocopying self-service.
No coins. First 5 pages free. Additional copies $.08/page. Microfilm reader/
printer. Copies .12/page. All correspondence answered. Limited research. Material may be borrowed through Interlibrary Loan request from any library in or
out of Vermont using standard ILL forms. ILL forms must be sent to the
Reference Services Unit (same address). Holdings include Vermont newspapers
(largest collection in the state); Federal Census for Vermont 1790-1900, including 1880 and 1900 Soundex indices; Vermont State Government publications; Vermontiana - "a major collection of books, periodicals, pamphlets, documents, etc.
about Vermont, its history, including county and town histories, its people and
its culture."

MONTPELIER - <u>VERMONT STATE PAPERS OFFICE</u> (Secretary of State)

26 Terrace Street   I-89 to Montpelier exit. Left at
(Redstone Building)   traffic light. Straight thru next
Montpelier, VT 05602   traffic light & bear left as going
802-828-2369   up the hill. Redstone at left at
Mon-Fri 7:45-4:30   top of hill.

Staff will arrange photocopying. No charge for first 20 pages. 20 copies or
more .05/page. No materials loaned. All correspondence answered. Limited
research. Will check name index, search for and send relevant material.
Holdings include manuscript Vermont state papers; a name index to the papers
circa 1740-1850, with scattering to circa 1880.

MONTPELIER - <u>VERMONT</u> <u>HISTORICAL</u> <u>SOCIETY</u> <u>LIBRARY</u>
      109 State Street (Pavilion Office Building)
      Montpelier, VT 05602   Red brick Victorian bldg, second
      802-828-2291   beyond Capitol on State St.
      Mon-Fri 7:45-4:30

The library is one unit of the Vermont Historical Society, which also maintains a museum. (See entry under <u>VERMONT</u> <u>-</u> <u>SOCIETIES</u>) Admission free. Photocopying done by staff only. .15/page, plus postage on mail orders (.50/25 pages). Limited reference by mail. Materials are not generally loaned. Holdings include a large genealogical collection; local history of New England as well as Vermont. The library of the <u>Vermont</u> <u>Society</u> <u>of</u> <u>Colonial</u> <u>Dames</u>, which includes the <u>American</u> <u>Genealogical</u> <u>and</u> <u>Biographical</u> <u>Index</u> (AGBI) is housed here.

POULTNEY - <u>GREEN</u> <u>MOUNTAIN</u> <u>COLLEGE</u> <u>LIBRARY</u>
      Poultney, VT 05764
      802-287-9313, Ext. 42 & 43
      Mon-Fri 8-5; 6:30-10:30; Sat 8-5; Sun 1:30-5, 6:30-10:30
      Summer: Mon-Fri 8-12, 1-4

Methodist Conference records (uncataloged); Journals and Yearbooks of the Conference; vertical files for each church in Conference - may be consulted with special permission. Inquiries by mail have low priority. When time allows, records will be searched. Fee: $3/hour.

RUTLAND - <u>RUTLAND</u> <u>FREE</u> <u>LIBRARY</u>
      Court Street   South on Rte 7 to Center Street.
      Rutland, VT 05701   Turn right. Library at corner
      802-773-1860 & 1861   of Center and Court.
      Mon-Thurs 9-9; Fri 9-5:30
      Sat 9-5. Summer closing Tues-Fri 5:30; Sat 5.

Self-service photocopying .10/page. 2 microfilm readers. All mail answered. Letters requiring extensive research may be referred to a local genealogist. Holdings include Rutland County census 1790-1910 (microfilm); <u>Rutland</u> <u>Herald</u> from 1792; Barbour Index to Connecticut Vital Records; DAR lineage books, Walton's registers, town reports from 1880, directories, Beers' atlases, plus a good collection of printed and microfilmed materials on Vermont and New England local history and genealogy in a locked room.

VERGENNES - <u>BIXBY</u> <u>MEMORIAL</u> <u>FREE</u> <u>LIBRARY</u>
      258 Main Street   North side of Rte 22 in
      Vergennes, VT 05491   center of town.
      802-877-2211
      Mon & Fri 12:30-8; Tues & Thurs 12:30-5; Wed 10-5

Staff-operated photocopying .10/page. One microfilm reader. Staff research limited to quick search of indexes or sources. Letter may be referred to local historian. Materials loaned on Interlibrary Loan on standard ILL forms. Holdings include a good collection of Vermontiana, small genealogical collection, local newspapers on microfilm, some back to 1850, DAR Patriot Index, War Rosters, Hemenway.

SOCIETIES

There are approximately 125 historical societies and related groups in Vermont. Most of them are small, with no headquarters or staff. They vary greatly as to their resources and interest. For a list of historical societies in Vermont consult the Directory of Historical Societies and Agencies in the United States and Canada, published by the American Association for State and Local History, or inquire about an individual local society at the Vermont Historical Society which maintains a more complete and up-to-date list of local groups.

GENEALOGICAL SOCIETY OF VERMONT

Joann Nichols, President
46 Chestnut Street
Brattleboro, VT 05301
802-254-9554

"Branches and Twigs"
Jean Harvie, Treasurer (1984)
P.O. Box 422
Pittsford, VT 05763

Founded October 1971 "to foster genealogical interest and activity, assemble, preserve, and make available genealogical records and to assist those in need of genealogical information and help."

Dues: $15 annual Oct./Oct. Meetings: Biannual. Third Saturday, May & October, Various locations. Publications: "Branches and Twigs" (Quarterly from Winter, 1972.) Some Vermont Ancestors: The Bicentennial Project of the Genealogical Society of Vermont. 83 pp. Order from Mrs. Nichols.

VERMONT HISTORICAL SOCIETY
(See address under VERMONT - LIBRARIES - MONTELIER)

The Vermont Historical Society was established in 1838. It maintains a library, a museum and administrative offices. Membership is $10 per year which includes a quarterly, "Vermont History," and a newsletter, neither of which is genealogical in nature.

****

BOOKS AND ARTICLES

Clark, Byron N., ed. A list of Pensioners of the War of 1812, 1904. Reprint, Baltimore, MD: Genealogical Publishing Company, 1969.

Eichholz, Alice. Collecting Vermont Ancestors. New Trails. Box 766, Montpelier, VT 1985.

Hanson, Edward W., "Vermont Genealogy: A Study in Migration," New England Historical and Genealogical Register, 133 (1979), 3-19, and in Genealogical Research in New England, Genealogical Publishing Co., 1984.

Hemenway, Abby M. <u>Vermont Historical Gazetteer</u>, (5 vols. 1867-1891), published at Burlington and other places.

Swift, Esther M., <u>Vermont Place-Names</u>: <u>Footprints of History</u>. Brattleboro, VT: Stephen Greene Press, 1977.

<u>Vermont Marriages, Vol I</u>: <u>Montpelier, Burlington, Berlin</u>, 1903. Reprint, Baltimore, MD: Genealogical Publishing Company, 1967.

U.S. Bureau of the Census. <u>Heads of Families of the United States taken in the Year 1790</u>: <u>Vermont</u>, 1907. Reprint, Baltimore, MD: Genealogical Publishing Company, 1975.

U.S. Bureau of the Census. <u>Heads of Families at the Second Census Taken in the year 1800</u>: Vermont, 1938. Reprint, Baltimore, MD: Genealogical Publishing Company, 1972.

****

INDEX